HI, JUST A QUICK QUESTION

MORROW
GIFT

HI, JUST A QUICK QUESTION

QUERIES, ADVICE, AND FIGURING IT ALL OUT

BETH EVANS

table of contents

hi, just a quick question

DEALING WITH PEOPLE...........50

SOCIAL ANXIETY......................82

ANXIETY

INTRODUCTION

I wrote this book during what might have been the most difficult time in my entire life.

Everything had been going so well. I had moved into my first solo apartment. I was excited to get to work on this book, excited for a whole bunch of concerts, events, and travels, and just generally excited for life. My friends and family were proud of me. For the first time in my life, I really felt like I had my life on track. Holding the keys to my apartment, I was so, so happy.

But life has a way of giving, and also taking. After this happy period, I experienced a lot of major upheaval in a very short time. A death in my family that affected me greatly— not because I missed the person, but because it had been an extraordinarily complicated, oftentimes horrible relationship. My eating disorder flared up, and every day became a battle where I felt like I was losing. This eventually led to my collapse alone in the apartment I loved. I felt overcome by the idea that everyone I loved was going to leave me. My cat died. And I had no idea how I was going to write this book. Every time I sat down to work on it, I kept thinking, "I am such a hypocrite. How can I possibly give advice when I'm falling apart at a thousand miles an hour? Who will event WANT to listen to me?"

So, to give advice, I took some age-old advice—write what you know. I know about sadness and anxiety and wanting to be literally anyone else on earth but myself. I know what it's like to be so desperate to change but to feel like a failure before even trying. And I know what it is like to sit in those emotional dark pits, the ones that consume every minute of your day.

In short, I wrote a lot of these sections to myself. I tried to write to myself as a friend, and I hope maybe you will find a friend in me as well. It's so incredibly hard wanting to pick yourself up but struggling every time you do so. I just want you to know you're not alone, that a lot of us feel lost, confused, hopeless, or worried to no end. We tend to write these off as bad feelings, but they're really just . . . feelings. They happen.

There's another side to all of this—a light at the end of the tunnel, if you will. I'm still trying to find it, and I hope you're trying too. Everything might not be sunshine and daisies, but I think there's something quite beautiful in really, honestly trying to make things better for yourself. I hope you'll join me in just trying. It might not be perfect, but I believe in you. I hope you believe in me too.

Daily Life

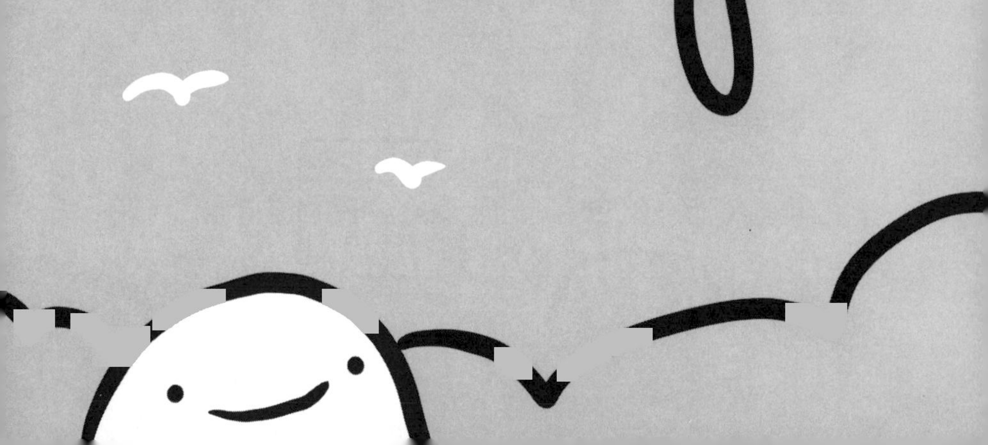

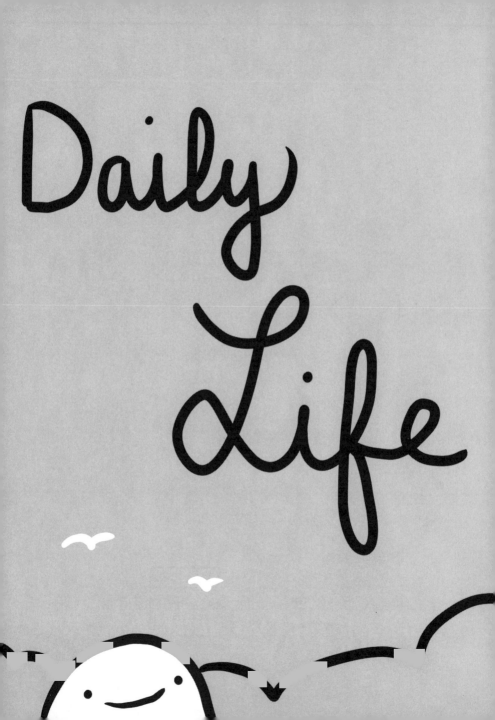

HOW DO I SURVIVE A NORMAL SCHOOL/WORK/DAY ROUTINE?

woohoo

TODAY

nothing special

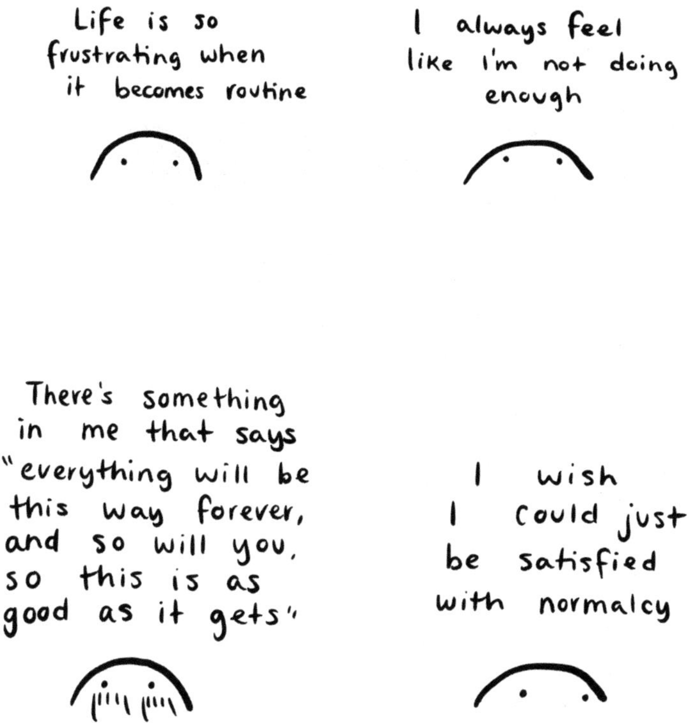
Life is so frustrating when it becomes routine
I always feel like I'm not doing enough
There's something in me that says "everything will be this way forever, and so will you, so this is as good as it gets"
I wish I could just be satisfied with normalcy

Personally, having something - anything, really, to look forward to - keeps me going. I like having plans in my back pocket.

They don't always have to be a big thing like a trip - sometimes just knowing I'll get to play Legend of Zelda with my best friend gets me through the biggest bummer of a week.

Having little things to look forward to can give you a much-needed motivation boost to get through everything. It doesn't have to be sheer mental willpower. It's okay to use motivators and rewards. This is an investment in you!

you seriously don't have to have "major problems" to struggle with getting through the week

if you struggle you struggle — it's OK

When there's little variation in routine it's super easy to feel stuck. And when we're stuck we feel anxious. It's OK. We can help break it up — but still get everything done.

try packing a different lunch or coffee

sometimes cheap new office supplies you use daily help too

give yourself a treat to look forward to when you get home - library books are my favorite

wear the most comfortable clothes you're allowed (or set them out for you to come home to!)

print off a picture you like for your planner

write your feelings down in a journal- daily logs will be fun to look back on!

There are bad days... and then there are days that are so perfectly ordinary and standard that they make us sad. It's like "wow, will it just be like this FOREVER?!?" That trapped-in-my-routine feeling can be impossible to shake.

this is so normal   I HATE IT

Everything feels like a chore! You can't stop watching the clock! There's nothing to look forward to later! It's also probably winter! All of these things can turn daily living into a thing of dread. And that can make just trying to live your life more difficult.

everything is fine but always the same

am I doing something wrong?

what if it gets worse?

is this how it will always feel?

am I stuck?

Sometimes the days feel like
a waiting game

Like nothing is happening, but
the days keep passing

It's okay - every day you are
here is totally awesome!

HOW DO I DO SOMETHING I WOULDN'T NORMALLY DO?

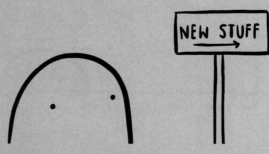

"I AGREED TO DO SOMETHING OUTSIDE MY COMFORT ZONE"

B I N G O

why did I say yes	(checks phone)	your watch is your best friend now	group chat	I hope there's a dog
dreading it the whole day	A BAR?!?	will require lying about interests	requires a skill	if I leave now, I can be home by...
frantic text to best friend	a whole planned outfit	FREE panic attack SPACE	at night ☆ ☾ ☆	(checks social media) (closes) (checks again)
I JUST WANT TO GO HOME!	requires a ticket	transportation planning is a must	worry all week about budget	you're someone's plus one
does everyone know each other except me?	maybe if I laugh no one will notice my misery	stand in corner holding drink the whole time	(mentally list all the things I could be doing instead)	internally AHHHH HHHHH HHHHH

I love enthusiastically making plans and then changing my mind two seconds later and then agonizing for weeks about what to do. Wait, no, I absolutely hate it.

oh NO!

TODAY
the thing!

Look, we all do it! We all overcommit and spend the whole event wishing we were doing anything else, and then tell everyone it was THE BEST. THING. EVER.

yeah it was sooooo great!

no I did not!

you cried the whole time in a corner?

yeah, I was there...

The truth is, we often feel compelled to say yes and attend everything. For me, all the years of being bullied and having no friends makes me feel like I **HAVE** to go to everything, or everyone will hate me and stop talking to me.

you are invited

friday @ 8pm

\# ATTEND OR WE HATE YOU AND WILL NEVER SPEAK TO YOU EVER AGAIN

sincerely, friends

it's amazing how we can still believe everyone dislikes us, even when we logically know everything is okay

Sometimes we need to pick and choose our battles with this feeling when we want to cancel everything. It's good to show up for the important stuff, like a friend's birthday bash. But you don't have to go to every bar and club night on Fridays. You're important too!

If you know a certain event is going to be too much, it's okay to say no!

PLANS

- meet up
- bar
- party   RELAX

COMMITTING TO STUFF

a contract with myself

1. I will go if it's mega-important
2. I will give myself permission to say no if I will be miserable the whole time
3. If I go to something that will make me miserable, I will not make everyone else miserable
4. I will not do stuff that's really outside my comfort zone (ie: drink), but I will explore healthy things, like talking to someone new
5. I will find other ways in my life to try new things in a less anxiety-provoking manner
6. I will be gentle with myself if I feel the outing wasn't successful

Okay cool! Good for you!

---

your name

I can't countersign, I have no legality, but it looks nice here

all night wild
P A R T Y

Not every event is going to be your cup of tea (which you wish you were home drinking)

It's cool, you're cool, and it will all (mercifully) be over soon!

HOW DO I DEAL WITH A BAD DAY?

Bad days suck. At their best, they're inconvenient, and at their worst, they last forever and it feels like nothing will ever be okay.

this feeling is the WORST →

Bad days often happen when we're already feeling down. They're another kick when we don't need it. And sometimes, when we're upset, it extends to others.

that kind of day, huh?

yeah

So yeah, no one enjoys them. And then we get caught up in the "tomorrow will be better" thing and feel pressure from that! You can survive a bad day – it's not fun, but it can be a little bit less painful.

WHAT WOULD MAKE THIS BETTER?

Sometimes identifying one thing that would either fix things or make them easier helps prioritize exactly what needs to be done, or provides a clearer idea of what to do.

If nothing comes to mind, or if the stuff that went wrong can't be fixed, it's time for:

WHAT WOULD MAKE ME BETTER?

You matter too! Keeping yourself going takes work, and you're worth the investment. Figure out what you need to get through the day.

you're important — promise!

BAD DAY BUSTERS

text someone you care about

watch a video of your favorite celebrity or musician

FUZZY SOCKS!

a nice cup of tea

stuffed animals

I REALLY DIDN'T THINK THIS THROUGH

a really good book

← please consider this one :,

face masks + skin care

good friends ♡

twinkling lights

WHEN IN DOUBT

Get some sleep!

It's okay - and healthy - to just want to hit the reset button. You'll feel better for it.

Sometimes it's just hard being human

Things that seem "basic" can be so difficult

And it's OK to acknowledge that and that you struggle - because we all struggle

You're going through a rough patch, but this will change - I hope it happens soon

HOW DO I HAVE A GOOD DAY?

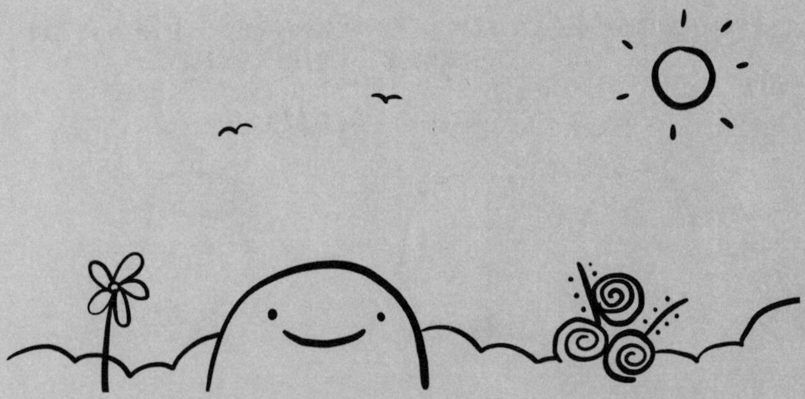

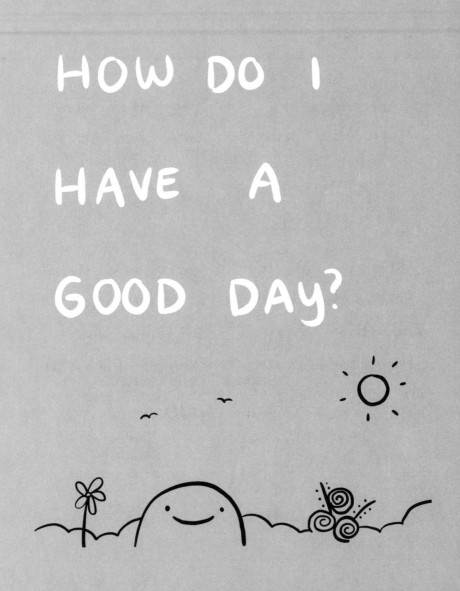

Wow, today was a
really good day and I
think things went well!

Okay so when do I feel
miserable again and
also everyone probably
hates me AND—

Crafting a good
day takes a lot of pressure off the
traditional "perfect day," and makes it
feel a lot more realistic and
achievable. Although good days can be
planned, they do spontaneously happen-
which also gives a better idea of how
to achieve them.

be prepared
for it to

be totally out
of nowhere-
you can't always
write them down
in advance!

I don't think you always need a
positive mindset going into it.
Some of my favorite days started
so miserable, but turned into
something else entirely - something
awesome. It's more important to be
open to the possibility of good than
forcing endless positivity.

WHAT MAKES A DAY GOOD FOR YOU?

Is it being surrounded by people...

... or being all by yourself?

Is it getting out and doing things...

... or staying inside and relaxing?

Is it getting a lot done...

... or not doing anything at all?

There's no right or wrong way to have a good day. But thinking about what you'd <u>like</u> to do in your free time helps shape it to be tailored to you. You can even sketch a rough plan for how your day might look!

don't be afraid to go along for the ride with unexpected events!

Just... be open to the possibility of a good day. It doesn't have to be nonstop sunshine and everything going great. But thinking "I am doing something I like, and I might enjoy this" can help shape the day, and leave you more open to other good stuff happening.

you've got this day!

thanks! you too!

There's definitely a real worry that if you have a good day, that's it - you will never have another good day. and it's just a waiting game until you feel miserable again.

But it's also good to have good days and remember how they feel, because they **will** help you get through those bad days - but also remind you there will be more of them.

HOW DO I HANDLE HOLIDAYS WHEN I'M LESS THAN CHEERY?

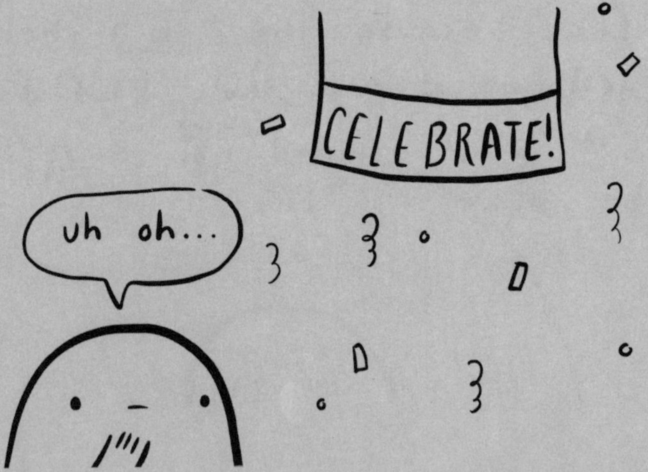

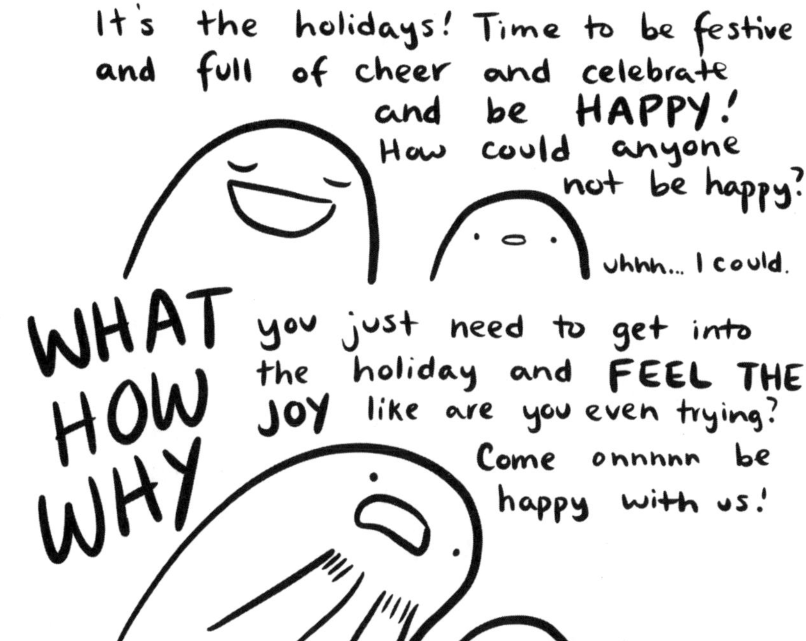
It's the holidays! Time to be festive and full of cheer and celebrate and be HAPPY! How could anyone not be happy?
uhhh... I could.
WHAT HOW WHY
you just need to get into the holiday and FEEL THE JOY like are you even trying? Come onnnnn be happy with us!
uh-
HOW CAN YOU NOT BE HAPPY?!?
Well, I think I found one of the reasons...

Sometimes when holidays and celebrations happen everyone expects us to be HAPPY! and CELEBRATORY! Which is mega hard, if you're struggling.

Those expectations can feel so awful.

Can't you get into the holiday spirit?

yeah just be happy

TOO.
MUCH.
PRESSURE.

It's downright impossible to <u>make</u> yourself have a good time, and that's okay. Sometimes it's healthier to cope, rather than celebrate. Forcing being happy just leads to misery. So be sad!

Hiding those feelings on the holidays makes it much worse!

PARTY →

While you might be OK with not celebrating, not everyone around you will get it.

BE A PART OF THINGS

CELEBRATE HOW ARE YOU SAD

COME ONNN IT'S THE HOLIDAYS! BE JOYFUL!

yikes!

It doesn't even matter if you explain why you're having a hard time - some people just have this fantasy that all holidays and celebrations are perfect. This is on them, not you. Be gentle with yourself around all the forced happiness and cheer.

You're doing just fine.

HOLIDAY SURVIVAL GUIDE

some quick tricks for some tough times

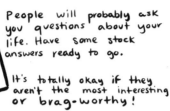

People will probably ask you questions about your life. Have some stock answers ready to go.

It's totally okay if they aren't the most interesting or brag-worthy!

enough about me HOW ARE YOU?

Deflect personal questions by asking people how they are doing! It shows interest in their life and lets someone else talk.

Sometimes people want a full explanation for why you aren't a ball of joy. You don't have to get totally into it. Some people don't get it, so try checking in with people who do, even if it's by text.

I'm having a hard time, but I'm trying. Thanks for your concern.

BUT—

Give in a little to stuff. You don't have to enjoy it, but smiling for someone's photo or trying a relative's cooking could really make their day. **Small gestures let people know** you really are trying, even though things are hard.

Head out and collect your thoughts.

You'd be surprised—someone might want to join you too. Breaks are healthy at events!

A holiday is just that -
a day

You will have many other
days to feel
happy

TOMORROW

HOLIDAY

And it will be on your
terms, when you are ready.

HOW DO I GET A GOOD NIGHT'S SLEEP?

A TYPICAL NIGHT'S SLEEP
(for those of us who can't)

11:00 PM

okay time for bed!

1:00 AM

I think I'm falling asleep...

3:00 AM

wait why am I awake WHY

3:42 AM

(Furiously Wikipedia search various historical events)

5:00 AM
Maybe I'm falling asleep again...

7:00 AM
I'm awake but mostly not

SLEEP IS FOR THE WEAK

...Or so I tell myself when I wake up in the morning after a completely exhausting night of tossing and turning. Spoiler alert: I don't sleep!

hey caffeine...

my buddy...

my pal...

It's totally wild to me that some people can just lay down and sleep, and not wake up and worry about every last detail in their life.

Oh I slept like a baby last night!

Me too, I woke up five times screaming.

Sleep is supposed to be restorative and you're supposed to wake up refreshed and ready to take on the day, but to me that's all lies!

how to sleep

- pee before bedtime, just do it, trust me
- leave your phone across the room (bonus: if you need alarms in the morning, you really have to get out of bed now)
- no clocks on your nightstand, you'll just obsess over **them**
- white noise or a fan can be super relaxing and drown out noises
- light-blocking sleep blindfolds trick you into thinking it's night and time to rest
- think about the temperature and plan accordingly with the right blankets
- comfy clothes!
- if you grind your teeth to nubs (like me) wear your mouthguard; your teeth will thank you (or be less angry in the day)
- give yourself a break, because sleep doesn't always come **easily!**

when you can't sleep

When you wake up and totally can't get back to sleep, it might be tempting to just lie there and force it.

Honestly, just getting up and doing something - anything, really — will make this less awful. I often get up and do boring stuff, like pay bills or organize things. It gives you a chance to be productive, and your body ultimately <u>will</u> let you know when it's tired.

Plus it saves you hours of lying there and agonizing about how you're just, well, lying there.

Relax!
why don't you
chill out and
get some sleep?   oh sure

Because lying here for
hours with my anxious
brain is   SO RELAXING

HOW DO I STOP PROCRASTINATING?

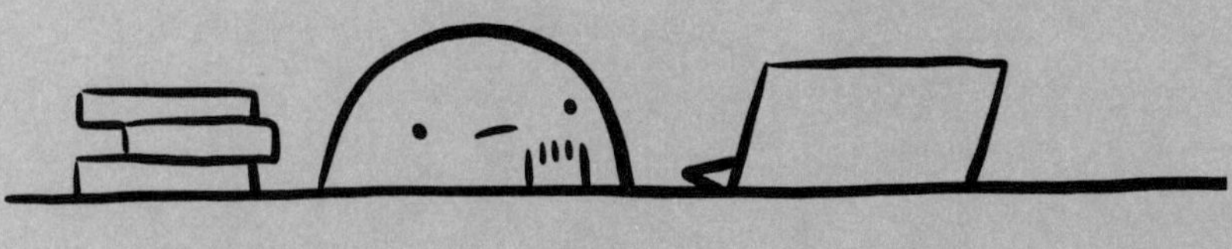

PROCRASTINATOR CYCLE

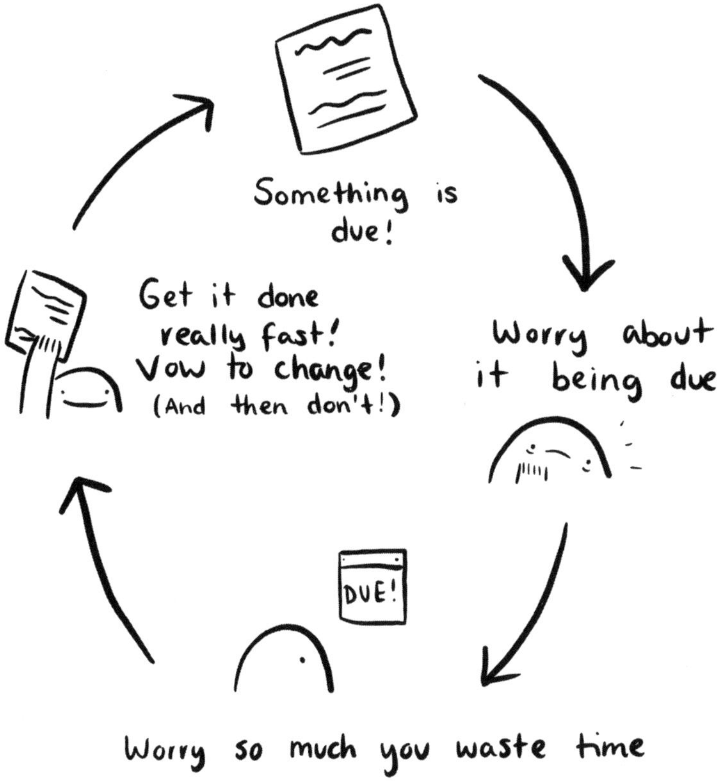
Something is due!
Worry about it being due
DUE!
Worry so much you waste time
Get it done really fast!
Vow to change!
(And then don't!)

I'm the kind of person who puts stuff off until the last minute, does everything in a rush, and calls it my "work style." I also make zero effort to change, even though I know it could be helpful.

deadline day

constant worry about quality of my work

drawing tablet charging from overuse

a mess of notes

Putting things off brings temporary relief, but makes things so much harder in the long run! And it can feel impossible to break out of this pattern. Like "Well I've always survived like this, guess I will keep it up!" Then late nights and a feeling of constant dread eat me up.

it's... FINE!

BREAK THE CYCLE

Prioritize what needs to be done and how much time you have. This should give you an idea of how many days you need, and the average amount per day. You don't have to meet all the targets, but knowing where you are weekly can relieve some stress.

Play to your strengths! Work on the pieces that you know you can do - it will make the harder stuff suck less, because you'll be warmed up from the work you knew you could finish. No one wants to sit down and have an impossible burden - but this can ease it a little bit. Divide and conquer, baby!

Break up the workload. Take a walk or run an errand. TV or reading can lead to getting off track - save them as a reward for the end of the day. Giving yourself time to clear your head can even help if you're super stuck on figuring a problem out!

Reach out to someone on the project! Ask questions, get clarity, and stress a little less. Talking to people not involved is good too, because you get a different perspective and new advice. But mostly you won't feel as isolated in getting everything done.

Give yourself a light at the end of the tunnel for getting everything done.

Sometimes we have to bribe ourselves to keep our sanity through stuff. Maybe there's a movie coming out, or a store you want to visit. For me, when I turn in this book, I'm playing Pokémon Sword and Shield (I'm starting Sobble!)

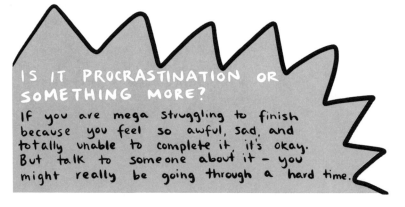

IS IT PROCRASTINATION OR SOMETHING MORE?

If you are mega struggling to finish because you feel so awful, sad, and totally unable to complete it, it's okay. But talk to someone about it — you might really be going through a hard time.

No one changes
overnight, and that's OK

Little bits at a time
are amazing!

(Try to turn your
work in on time!)

HOW DO I STAY MOTIVATED IN LIFE IN GENERAL?

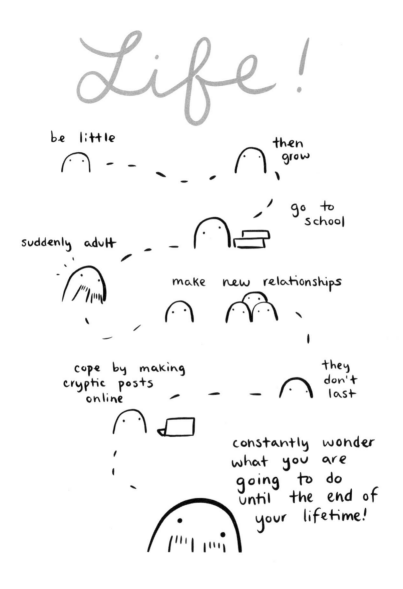

Life!

be little — then grow

go to school

suddenly adult — make new relationships

cope by making cryptic posts online — they don't last

constantly wonder what you are going to do until the end of your lifetime!

motivation

Even when things are going kind of well, being human is hard! And trying to keep up with living the life of a functioning person is actually really difficult!

it's like they all want my attention!

Losing your motivation is the worst, because you don't feel emotionally invested or connected, and like a failure for not caring more. You definitely aren't a failure, but you may be burning out.

Burnout can happen to anyone — and not just in your work life.

It's not that you don't care— you just care so much that it's competing for attention in your life with, well, everything.

burned out

We've all tried to do too much before, even if we don't realize it. Taking on the world can make us less excited to live in and enjoy it.

I am incapable of feeling joy

Scaling back isn't the end of the world. Prioritizing what needs to be done should also allow time for you. It isn't weak - it's totally healthy.

I'm going to get through this...

Give yourself a break - and a little time to get your spark back. You'll feel more energized to keep going ahead. Be kind to yourself!

ways to stay motivated

Look back at the reasons you like doing certain things. Is it the people? The self-satisfaction? What actually makes you want to take the time to stay involved? It's okay if the answer is money- we all need to live. But if something keeps you going, it's sometimes nice to remember.

We all have to do stuff we don't want to do. For example, right now I'm trying to be creative on a deadline but all I want to do is look up videos of anteaters. (I LOVE EVERYTHING ABOUT THEM.) Sometimes setting small rewards, like " I can look up good anteater content IF I finish this section first" gives you something more fun to work toward. It's like an immediate reward!

I FINE DID IT

GET IT DONE!
1. WORK
2. CHORES
3. STUFF?

Breaking down what absolutely has to be done can help prioritize and organize the not-so-fun stuff in life, and make it a little easier to accomplish.

HOW TO PRIORITIZE

Whenever I went through a horrible time and felt like I couldn't do, like, anything, my dad had me make lists of what <u>had</u> to be done so I didn't stop functioning completely. Let's do one!

① YOU
yes, you! Make sure you're showering and doing hygiene. Seems basic but can be hard. It's a great step! Give yourself space to feel things, but also time to take care of yourself.

② DO IT (OR ELSE)
This is the kind of stuff like school or work that has due dates or other things you committed to. Keeping them can help you feel focused + involved.

③ SOCIAL
Try to see people, even if it's hard. Closing yourself off is easy, letting other people draw you back into life is hard. But worth it.

you're on my list

you're on mine too!

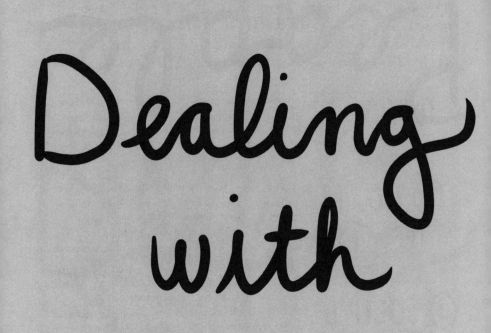

Dealing with

People

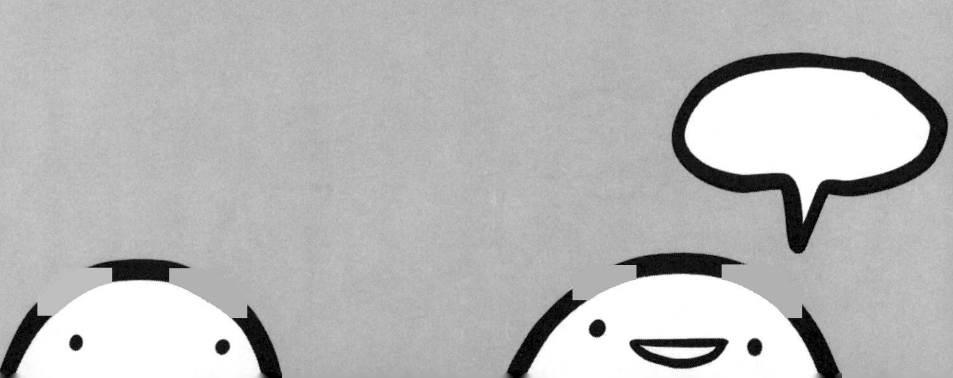

HOW DO I DEAL WITH DIFFICULT PEOPLE?

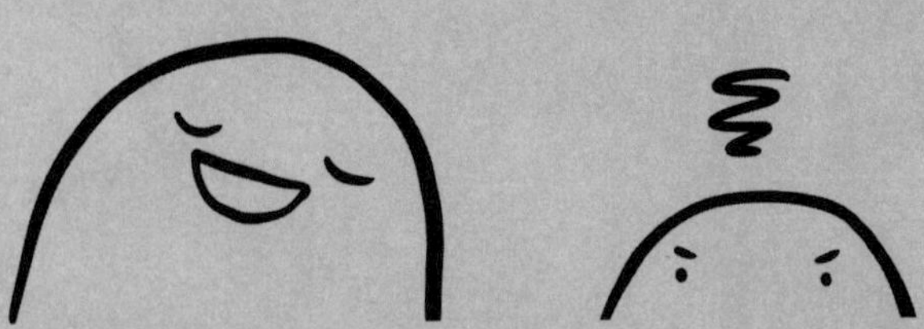

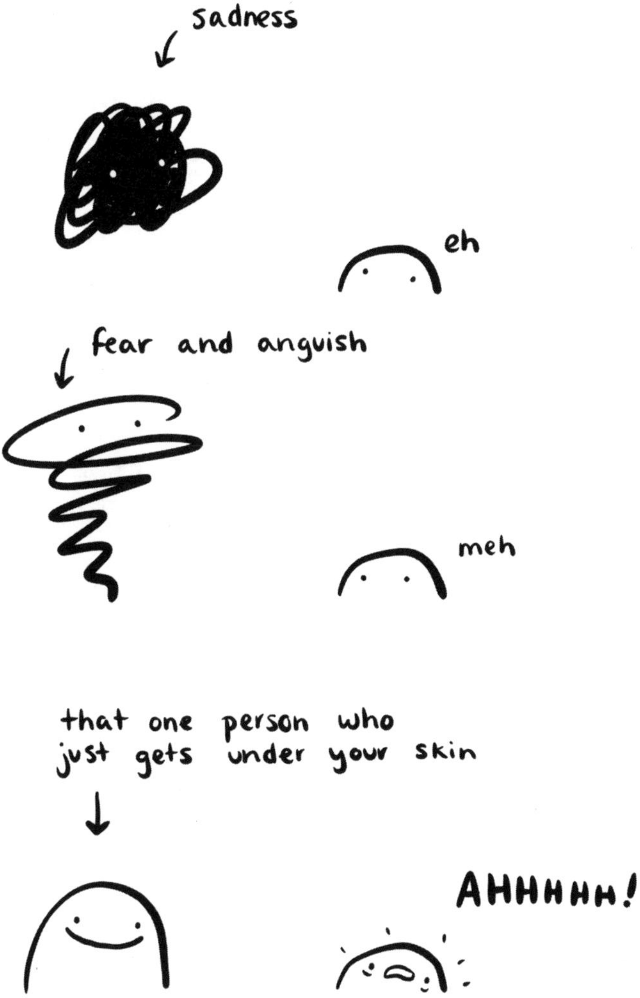
sadness
eh
fear and anguish
meh
that one person who just gets under your skin
AHHHHH!

As much as we act like we're good with everyone, there will inevitably be people that we just **DO NOT** get along with. It happens, and isn't a reflection on you.

the
know-it-all

the
mean guy

the "I never know WHAT I will get with them"

There are difficult people in all parts of life. Maybe they're random strangers, a classmate or co-worker, or even someone we are related to. And it can be hard, especially if we are really trying to connect with them. It makes us feel like we did something wrong. It's okay to not be best friends with everyone on Earth.

THE single most difficult person

Sooo... what should I do about those best friends forever bracelets...

WHY PEOPLE ARE DIFFICULT

attention

Some people just thrive on being noticed. Good or bad, just having someone have to spend their time being involved with them is important. High drama always seems to happen.

Cruelty

And some people are just mean because they can be. They thrive on making other people look or feel bad. And sure, they probably have problems of their own, but it's no excuse for being so mean. But still they persist, and it's so frustrating.

Cluelessness

? ? ?

Finally, sometimes people have no idea what's going on, making everything around them as chaotic as they are. Maybe they don't realize how their words or actions impact others — but it totally does.

AND HOW TO DEAL WITH THEM

ignore

Sometimes just acting like you
care about their difficult drama
and letting your mind wander
can really work.
It kind of feels like
letting them win, but keeping your
own sanity is a win too. Try to
keep their antics out of your
personal time, or they can consume!

remove

Although there are difficult people
we can't totally divorce ourselves
from, working to minimize our time
and interactions with them can be
healthy. And if you can't
remove yourself, try emotionally
removing yourself so it's
easier to get through their
interactions.

nudge

If they're clueless about how
their behavior affects other people,
clue them in! It could go well or
not, but trying shows you care about
them and how their actions are
perceived. Be gentle with it.

People can be difficult.

We can be difficult too.

Learn what you can from them
and yourself, and be the least
annoying person on the planet!

HOW DO I DEAL WITH PEOPLE WHO DON'T RESPECT PERSONAL BOUNDARIES?

YOU'VE SEEN THESE HORRORS

I'm a hugger!
You can't escape mine!

I'm going to ask
you a bunch of
invasive personal
questions!

I touch you
first and then
ask "is that okay?"

I'll misuse social
media until you're
so uncomfortable
you'll want
to quit!

NIGHT OF NO BOUNDARIES!

I think sometimes we feel like we
need excuses for not wanting
someone crossing our boundaries.

I can't hug,
uh... I'm sick?

You should never feel bad about
being uncomfortable with someone
crossing your personal boundaries!
Your boundaries are what you feel
comfortable with. And unfortunately,
not everyone notices, or even respects
them, until they've crossed them.
And then it becomes a huge messy
thing that feels weird because you
feel bad no matter how you speak up.

too close
too close
TOO CLOSE!

You have the right to dictate what you're comfortable with without shame.

But figuring out how to set those boundaries can be tricky - sometimes you're not even totally sure what you need, or would be useful. I think it helps to divide them into physical boundaries and emotional boundaries.

PHYSICAL

How do I want people to physically interact with me?

Am I OK with touching?

What parts of my body am I comfortable with being touched?

EMOTIONAL

How much do I want people to know about me?

What questions am I OK with people asking?

What pushes me too far with sharing, or with comments about me?

PHYSICAL

You **have** to be very clear, even if you feel like an asshole. Don't stress it, though. Finding your voice on this issue can be very empowering. Don't stop using it!

Sorry, I'd prefer not to hug, thanks!

← don't follow with a question like "if that's OK" because people WILL fight you on it

EMOTIONAL

This is a little tricky, because people can't always see how their words affect you. Again, it helps to be clear, like, "I'm not comfortable discussing that." But if people can't accept that, try showing how their words make you feel, ie "When you ask me that, it doesn't make me comfortable."

Of course, some people will continue to trample your boundaries — try limiting your time with them. It's OK to put yourself first.

I'd rather not talk about that.

It's okay to decide what you are comfortable with, and to live your life according to that

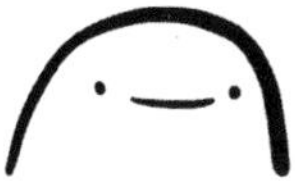

Some people might have their own boundaries, but hold on to the ones that matter – and to the people who understand, respect, and embrace both you and your boundaries

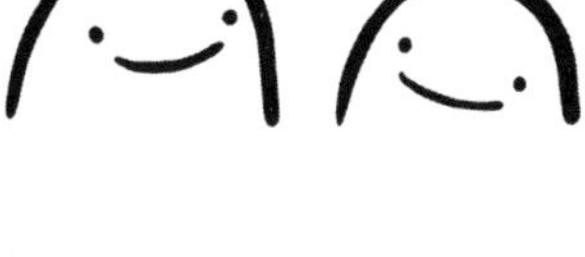

HOW DO I DEAL WITH FIGHTING WITH SOMEONE?

point

counter-
point

surprise!

Flash
of anger!

annoyance

disappointment

upset

frustration

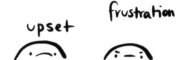

statement
of
regret

shock!

mad

mad

upset

very
upset

For me, one of the worst feelings in the world is fighting with someone. Stranger or friend, I absolutely HATE it. I avoid confrontation at all cost. Fighting makes me want to admit defeat for the sake of keeping the peace.

them, angry

me, hating this

I SURRENDER DON'T HATE ME OKAY?

Like it or not, conflict is a part of life. We butt heads with people or flat out get into it with them. Even people like me who despise conflict have had their share of what feels like end-of-the-world arguments.

I hate being dragged into fighting and I don't really like feeling angry - it's just an uncomfortable emotion I have trouble dealing with. which is OK.

Reluctant Participant

But sometimes arguments have to happen. They can be beneficial, like finally getting to a touchy issue in a relationship, or standing up for something you really believe in. Arguing sucks, but if you can turn it into something beneficial, it won't feel like such a waste of time.

oh you want to learn something from this? what did you learn?

to get new friends

Definitely pursue making up if the relationship is important to you. (please use good judgment if the relationship is healthy or not!) It takes strength to admit faults and work through what happened. But most of the time arguments are really goofy and petty anyways.

oh man that was awful, let's never do it again

YES!

FIGHTING ONLINE

I hate thisssss!

There is a **LOT** of fighting online, and even though it isn't in person, being involved or just watching it unfold can be totally anxiety-inducing.

It's easy to say "just log off/disengage" but much harder to actually do.

I don't argue with people who try to start fights with me. Partly because I don't know them, it's not worth it, they are just lashing out, etc. But mostly it's because it will make me so anxious I can't focus on anything else. You really don't have to engage with everyone if it causes you to disengage from your life. ↙ it's OK to just shut it off

Fighting with someone with a character limit isn't really fun. So don't do it if it's going to leave you in a bad place. Remember: private profiles are there for a reason- don't be afraid to use one.

PRIVATE

fights last

but a good friendship
can last forever

fight for what matters

HOW DO I LET PEOPLE HELP ME?

I'm here if you need anything.
Like at all. You can talk to me.

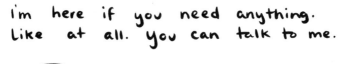

Okay, well,
actually—

Yeah this
is too much

SAME!

There are a lot of reasons why
we might not want to let other
people help us when we're struggling:

Maybe we're afraid
they won't understand
our problems.

Maybe we're worried
because we've asked
for help in the past,
and it hasn't gone well.

Maybe we're the kind
of people who do
everything ourselves,
and think we should
tackle all our problems
totally alone.

And maybe we're just
scared, because we
don't know how to
verbalize what's
going on.

Communication is tricky. Communication about mental health is HARD. It requires you to be at your most vulnerable, and you don't always know how anyone will react.

are you doing okay?

I... er... um... yeah?!?

it will be very tempting to lie

Something that takes some of the pressure off is knowing that you, and the person listening, will fail. I know! But knowing that not every interaction will be pure therapeutic bliss keeps things more real.

I don't get why you don't just do it differently?

are you even listening to me?

↖ oooh yeah this really hurts

Here are some things to keep in mind:

It doesn't matter if someone is a doctor or your mom. Anyone has the chance to be super helpful, or super hurtful. No one is perfect, but people can be, well, people!

Sometimes you have to "train" people with what does and doesn't work.

It's hard!

But be vocal, say how you're really feeling (which is scary) and be honest. It will go a long way in communication, and even further in being understood.

this doesn't help me because...

It is so easy to act like everything is okay. But it's so important to let people in however you can. No one should face huge burdens alone, and having the courage to confide in someone is so brave. Let people help you. Let them into your world. It will be imperfect and messy and agonizing...

... but so freeing.

let others help you

to help untangle all
the things consuming you

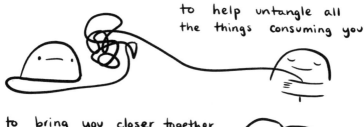

to bring you closer together
than you ever were before

to know you don't have to
face your demons alone

to know that someone truly cares — that's
a powerful thing, and perhaps the most
important tool in your kit for getting better!

HOW DO I HELP SOMEONE ELSE GOING THROUGH A HARD TIME?

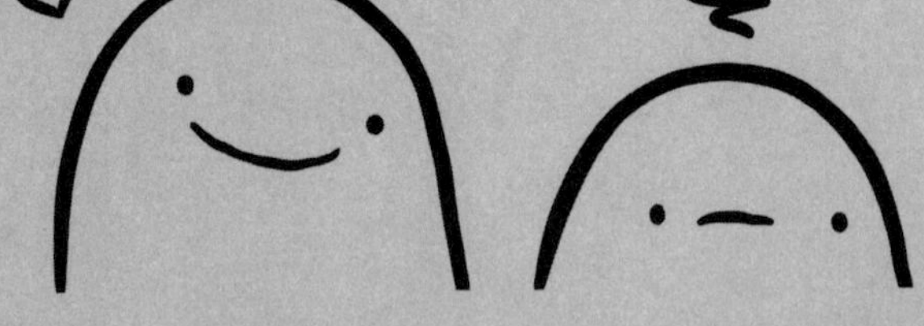

When you've been through some hard times, and maybe even shared what it's like, people might turn to you if they are also struggling.

hey, can we talk?

OH GOD
WHAT DO I DO

While it's great that they can trust you, you might feel a little caught off guard, unsure of what to do, and maybe even really freaked out about how to help them.

I'm a person!
Not a doctor!
What if my advice is TERRIBLE?!?

I think sometimes it's scary because in our head it's this:

GIVE ME ADVICE FOR MY COMPLEX ISSUES

But usually it's more like this:

hey, can I talk to you without fear of being judged?

Something that helps me freak
out a little less is trying to
remember what I found
UNHELPFUL when I was
struggling, and then I do
the exact opposite.

hmmm... talking
over me and
telling me what
to do didn't help.

I'll try listening!

Remember: you can never go
wrong with open ears and
an open heart!

... and that's
why I'm upset!

that sounds
hard

BE SURE TO VALIDATE

that's hard

Let them know their feelings are valid and okay to feel - whatever the feeling is.

DON'T BE BOSSY

Telling someone what to do is like the worst. If they want advice on how to handle a situation, they will explicitly ask.

BE PRESENT

it was awful!   it sounds awful!

Show that you're paying attention to what they are saying by echoing their sentiments. It's a nice way to show you are there and listening besides staring at them with a blank face.

FOLLOW THEIR LEAD

I don't want to go out!

That's okay, let's do something else

Pay attention to what seems fun, but also difficult to them. Maybe going out is stressful, so plan a night in. Or maybe a certain activity makes them happy - give it a go!

Keep in contact. Send them a picture, or a funny thing that reminds you of them. All the little things that show you care really add up!

COMMUNICATE

this made me think of you

LISTEN

!?!

This seems like a no-brainer, but taking the time to show interest in someone who feels vulnerable and like they aren't doing their best is the nicest thing you can do.

Social

Anxiety

HOW DO I MAKE FRIENDS AS AN ADULT?

Making friends at any **age** can be tricky - opening up is hard too!

But there are a lot of neat ways you can meet new people

Taking a class helps you meet people and try something new at the same skill level as everyone. I did improv, made new friends, and now I annoy them!

There are loads of online groups for specific interests and activities in your area - it's a fun way to explore your passions and do so with new people!

Online friends are real friends too! I have internet friendships from junior high I still keep up with! Send someone a message and get the ball rolling. (but be safe, okay?)

If you already have a friend, ask them to hang out with one of _their_ friends. You'll have a mutual buffer person and stuff to talk about.

If you aren't quite ready to let new people in, that's okay too.

Sometimes just going outside and getting coffee or going to the library and being around people is a great step forward!

MAKING NEW FRIENDS: DO'S AND DONT'S

DO take an interest in what the other person is saying - you can always parrot it back if you get stuck

it's so cool you collect gemstones but also found a portal to another dimension

thanks

DON'T choose conversation topics that might be off-putting, or cut the conversation short

gemstones are kinda ugly and this dimension is the best

uh?

DO ask plenty of questions! It shows an interest in the person and you learn more about them! (also you don't have to talk about yourself!)

what's your favorite gem?

is the portal safe?

how are you so cool?

oh! Well...

DON'T completely ignore what they say and jump into your own stuff and cut them off

OK COOL HERE'S EVERYTHING THAT HAS EVER HAPPENED WITH ME

oh... well...

DO realize that you might not hit it off with everyone, and friendships take time to develop

Hey, I was going to this thing next week, if you want to come that is cool!

sure!

DON'T endlessly beat yourself up if you didn't click — think of it as training for getting to know new people who fit with you better!

maybe next time!

HOW DO I MAKE PLANS

(AND NOT TOTALLY DREAD THEM?)

great! I
will be there

or I will cancel

or be there

or run away and cry

wait no I will TOTALLY be there

I think

We've all been there. We've made plans to do something, and then the day of it, we just want to cancel and stay home - even if we have been looking forward to it for weeks. There's just this overwhelming need to ESCAPE!

get me out
of here!

PLANS

I personally think it comes down to it being a commitment, and something in our brains going "there's no way to escape!" We feel so trapped, and then guilty because we <u>chose</u> to do this in the first place. And doubly guilty if other people are involved. The whole thing can be a bit too much.

do I go or cancel

go or cancel

go or cancel

HOW TO MAKE PLANS

Okay great! You want to do things and be out and about. Here's how to do that:

① Initiate, accept, or just confirm you will be going / attending

wanna go?

② Write it down or log it so you remember

friday EVENT!

③ Mentally put it in a box. Maybe you will go. Maybe you won't. You can make that call the day of the plans. Remind yourself you <u>always</u> can change your mind.

EVENT

④ Make your choice the day of the event. Know you have an out. Take comfort in your exit strategies, okay?

DON'T GO *GO*

HOW TO KEEP THEM

①

Distract yourself the day of the plans. Don't look at the clock too much or play "I only have ___ hours until I go!" Because it's super anxiety-inducing.

② *in case of emergency*

Have an emergency bag full of your medications, food, or even small trinkets you find comforting. It's like having instant backup.

③ EVENT

Try going for just a little. Not every event will be awesome, but the more you go to things, the easier they do get.

④

happy?
anxious?
upset?

T*even bad feelings can be useful*

No matter if you stayed or left, note your reactions for future use. It will help you figure out what things you'd like to do in the future!

Life is full of plans

Sometimes they go off course

You'll figure out how to steer
back on course — a course you
like and feel comfortable with

HOW DO I TALK IN FRONT OF PEOPLE I DON'T KNOW?

I HATE TALKING
IN FRONT OF STRANGERS

It doesn't matter if I'm prepared or winging it - I'm the kind of person who totally freaks out having to talk in front of three people I <u>do</u> know.

This is because
I HATE ATTENTION.

why are you all staring at me

uhhh because you're supposed to be talking?

It's like I totally forget everything I was going to say. At times like this I really want the earth to open up and swallow me.

Somehow this is an improvement

But as much as I'd like to never address groups of people ever again, it's a part of life we have to do. So here is everything I have learned, from book talk disasters to late night stand-up comedy. (yeah, I'm _that_ "guy.")

KNOW YOUR CROWD

Addressing people with anxiety let me tap into my own fears. Understanding your audience will give you an idea of how to present yourself — think of it as an acting challenge.

FAKE CONFIDENCE

Your audience will be as confident as you are. I did a stand-up class to get better at public speaking. cried all the time. I went out with a "how can this be any worse than what's in my head" attitude and survived.

CRACK A JOKE

This seems a little risky, but if you make light of you being nervous, people respond well because it makes you human. Don't make fun of the audience — just you!

IGNORE YOUR BODY

You're probably feeling a thousand kinds of uncomfortable, like sweating, nausea, or rising panic. Pick anything else in the room and focus on that.

NO ONE CARES

Seriously, people rarely remember this stuff, no matter if it's a one off speech in a class or a bunch of people listening at a party.

YOU WILL SURVIVE

It will feel weird and like it lasts forever, but also like it's over too soon. But you <u>can</u> do this and you <u>can</u> get through this!

IF YOU MESS UP

Okay, so mistakes can **AND** will happen.

In my stand-up class we had to practice hosting a show and addressing the crowd. I did so badly I managed to insult like all six people in the room and I had to leave to go cry in the bathroom.

Failing at public speaking ultimately makes you better at it, because what you did wrong is FOREVER burned in your brain and you will never do it again. It will suck big time to mess up, whether you trip up on words, forget stuff, or accidentally make fun of everyone's hobbies to the point that your instructor covers his face and asks "why'd you do that?" (Again... sorry Bryan)

you'll survive this, promise!

MADE A MISTAKE!

I'm awful!

PUBLIC SPEAKING AWARDS

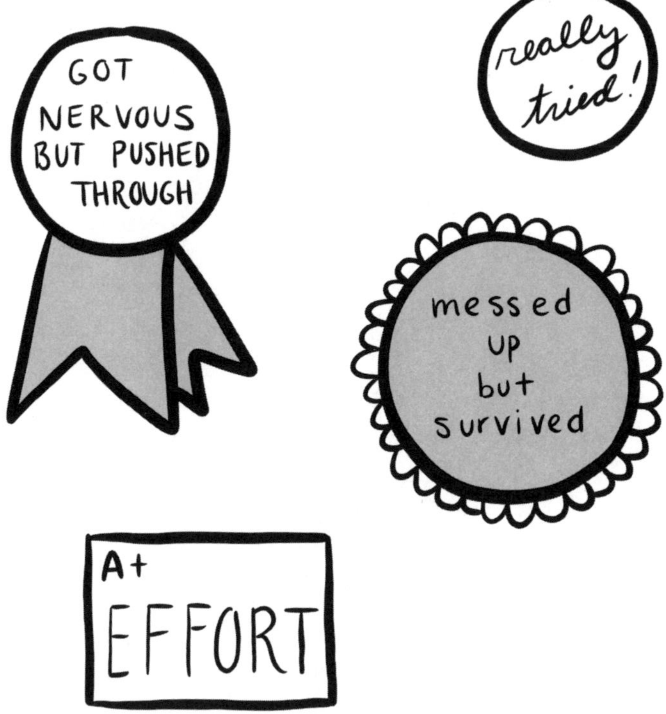
GOT NERVOUS BUT PUSHED THROUGH
really tried!
messed up but survived
A+ EFFORT

HOW DO I DEAL WITH A PANIC ATTACK IN PUBLIC?

If you've ever had a panic attack outside your home, it's probably felt like everyone is watching you

But chances are everyone around you is too involved in their own lives to notice, and your brain is making it a lot worse

I'M GETTING MY ANXIETY UNDER CONTROL I SWEAR

who are you?

what?

uhhh... why are you acting like that

I dunno...

... it's almost like you're upset or something?

wow what gave it away?

AND IF SOMEONE DOES NOTICE, THEY MIGHT SURPRISE YOU — SOMETIMES PEOPLE ARE GREAT

hey, are you okay?

LET'S CALM DOWN

if possible, find an exit

OUT →

if not, try to find a quiet, private place

try doing a small mental task, like counting to 15 or naming countries

3... 4... 5...

give yourself a chance to be in the moment — check out where you are

see if you can send a quick text to someone who understands

I'M UPSET!

If nothing works, look up pictures of animals

oh great I'm
panicking and
everyone is looking

and they're probably
like "why is that
person acting like
that" and they think
I'm super weird and a
loser and-

NOTHING TO
SEE HERE! IT'S
ALL GOOD!

who
are you?

what?

you are so
much more
than a
panic attack ♡

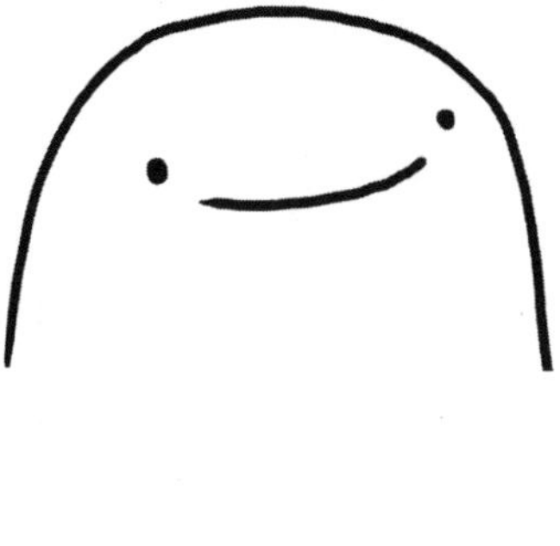

HOW DO I TAKE A COMPLIMENT?

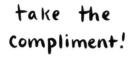

take the
compliment!

no

take the
compliment

no

TAKE!
THE!
COMPLIMENT!!!

ABSOLUTELY
NOT

Oh, compliments. Such a well-intentioned thing can turn into such an anxiety-provoking event. Someone just wants to tell us we did something well, and all we can do is think "I don't deserve this at all!"

you did a good job!

... can I go, please?!?

Here is what I tend to do when someone compliments me:

1. surprise

2. stammer of thanks

3. embarrassed for some reason?

4. self-doubt

Here is what you should do:

oh, thank
you

See, compliments are about us, but they're also about the person giving them. People like to be thanked. And by saying thank you, you don't have to agree with them. You are moving the conversation along, and hopefully the focus off of you. It's a win-win.

But do try examining what they complimented. Accepting one doesn't mean you're full of yourself. It means you did something right. Test it out - it might be a nice surprise.

♡?

so, you're
a compliment?

♡ yes

and you're
a good thing?

♡ yep!

♡

don't tell
anyone I'm here
with you

 ♡ I won't!

Compliments are good!

It's okay if you aren't ready to fully embrace them.

They're just a sign you are doing things right.

Keep up the good work, and maybe give one to someone else!

Anxiety

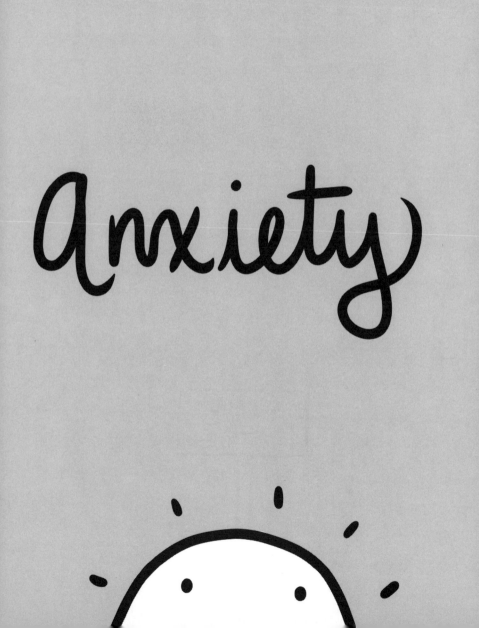

HOW DO I HANDLE SECURITY MEASURES AT EVENTS WHEN IT MAKES ME REALLY NERVOUS?

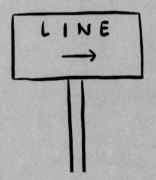

PLACES WITH SECURITY

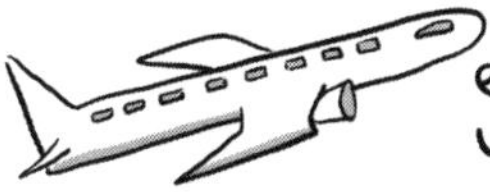

filled exclusively with screaming children

airplanes + airports

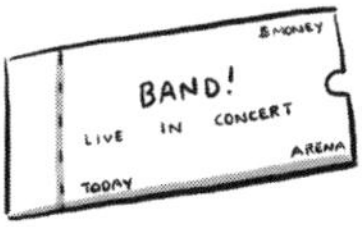
$MONEY
BAND!
LIVE IN CONCERT
TODAY
ARENA

your favorite artist here

concerts

standard sports imagery

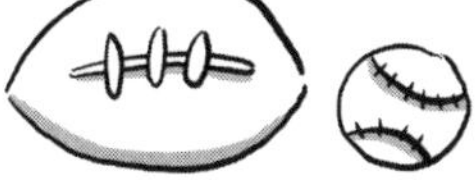

sports

lots of people

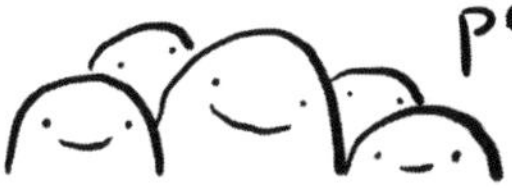

Large gatherings

It's not unusual or weird to get a little freaked out by them

(okay - or a <u>lot</u>)

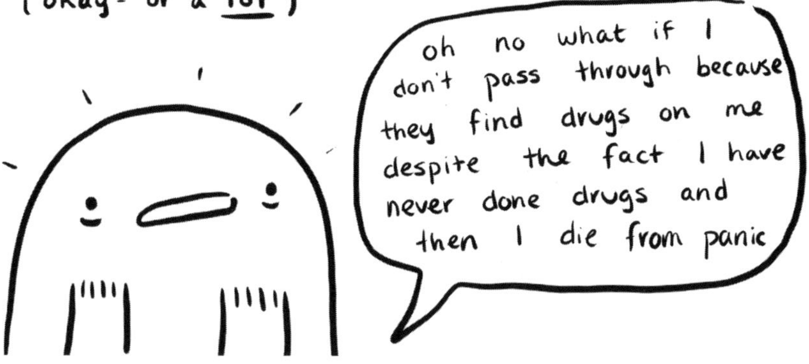
oh no what if I don't pass through because they find drugs on me despite the fact I have never done drugs and then I die from panic

SOME THINGS TO REMEMBER

going with someone, rather than alone, can make you feel more confident and a little bit safer

check the venue's bag policies - a small clear purse will get you into almost anywhere, and make passing through security quicker

if the metal detector goes off, it's probably just something minor, like your glasses or forgetting to take your keys out - you are not going directly to jail

oftentimes our anxious thoughts make it seem much worse than it really is

PATDOWNS

Sometimes you might be randomly selected for a physical patdown. These can be anxiety-inducing for a lot of reasons- often very, very personal ones. But you <u>can</u> get through it.

if you came with someone, try to see if they can be present - making eye contact can make you feel less alone

you have the right to have someone of the same gender perform it - don't be afraid to ask!

deep breaths help

in and out

so does remembering <u>why</u> you're doing this

I'm going to see them play live!

If you end up crying, it's not the end of the world. It's a normal reaction to something super anxiety-inducing. Some people might understand it and be sympathetic, others might not. But <u>you</u> understand why, so cut yourself some slack!

A NIGHT OUT + MY ENERGY

getting there

waiting in line

at the event

headed home

ready for bed

can't sleep!

A SMALL MANTRA

I am here

I **want** to do this

It's okay if I don't do
it totally perfectly

I am going out and
experiencing things

If I go home now it's
okay, because this does not
define me as a person

HOW DO I USE THE INTERNET WHEN IT GIVES ME ANXIETY?

This is the internet. Sometimes it is your best friend.

And sometimes it's your enemy.

Even when we know it's making us upset, sad, or miserable, we can't look away. It's like watching the world implode in real, up-to-the-minute time.

Have you ever seen someone get attacked on social media, and if you didn't automatically agree, you were some kind of horrible person? I think there's this really big fear that if you aren't ~~totally~~ perfect, say the right thing every time, and consume media that is "perfect," you deserve to have nothing good in the world. And that is SCARY. The fear of accidentally saying the wrong thing is so real and anxiety provoking for me that I've considered quitting altogether at times. And it's my job!

SHAME

BAD

So often people are like:

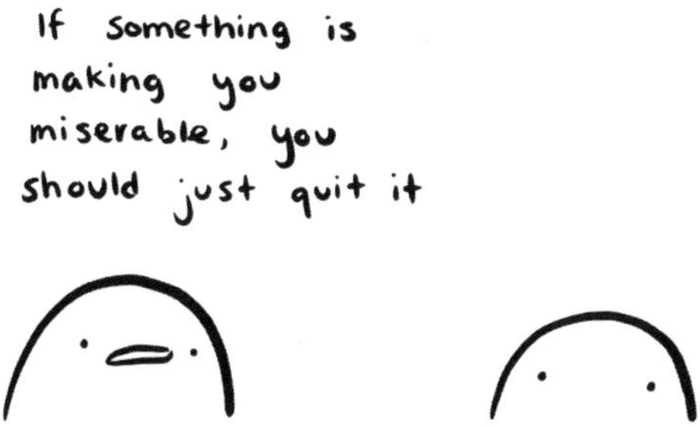
If something is making you miserable, you should just quit it

But that's the thing! It's the internet! You can't just never use the internet ever again! Striking that balance between using it and not going totally crazy seems downright impossible. A lot of us totally build our lives online, and the separation between online life and real-world life seems blurred. The point is, it's tricky.

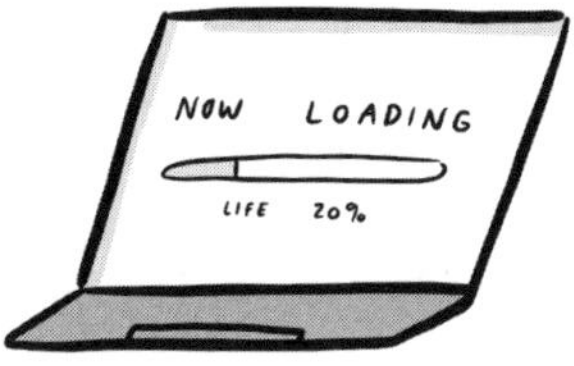
NOW LOADING
LIFE 20%

 Here is a guide to

surviving online

 OPINION
_____
_____
_____

Sometimes sharing your opinion on social media can be tempting.
But even your best intentions can backfire, because the internet is terrible. Sometimes staying away from opinion based sharing is healthy.

If you really love something but you're afraid of being judged, try scrapbooking about it instead. The only opinion you'll hear is your own - because it's a space just for you!

And if the internet is really driving you nuts, it's okay to sign out of your accounts and just breathe. It doesn't have to be forever - sometimes a few hours without seeing your news feed actually feels pretty good.

You know how people are like "no phone 30 minutes before bed"? Yeah, not going to happen. But maybe try picking something nice to look at instead of the constant drama of the world.

Don't be afraid to have locked or private accounts. It's actually super freeing controlling who sees your stuff. You'll feel more comfortable sharing and there's a far less likely chance a stranger will want to pick a fight with you.

Spend some time with people in the real world.

People communicate differently in person than they do online - especially when it comes to disagreements. It's a lot easier to share what you're thinking when there isn't a character limit and surprisingly less overwhelming.

And remember:

You are more than your social media.

You are a whole person!

HOW DO I TAKE CRITICISM WHEN I THINK I CAN'T DO ANYTHING RIGHT?

uh oh

CRITICISM CYCLE

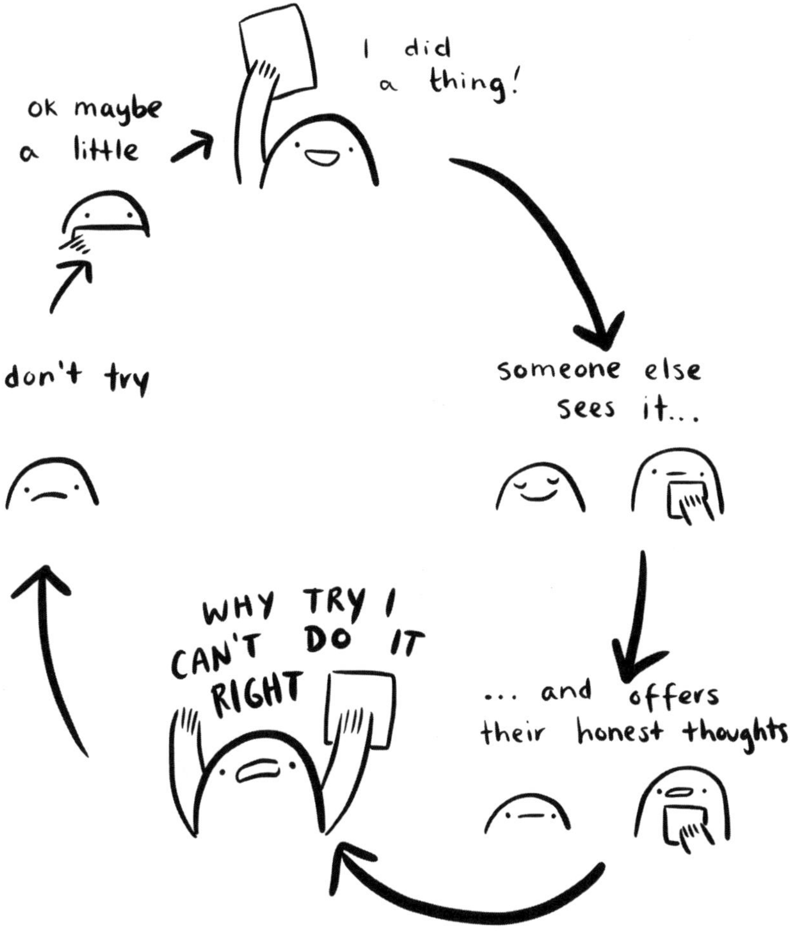
I did a thing!
someone else sees it...
... and offers their honest thoughts
WHY TRY I CAN'T DO IT RIGHT
don't try
ok maybe a little

Criticism can be tough and exhausting.
Not because I think everything I do is
amazing and perfect, but because I often
think I can't do anything right, criticism
reinforces it.

wow I
am terrible

I mean, we all receive criticism, both in
a constructive (like in an academic or
professional sense) and non-constructive
(people... yelling online?) manner. And it's
so easy to get totally wrapped up and
never want to try anything again.

personally,
I take
everything,
well...
    personally

and I
WILL
CRY

The key is figuring out if the person who is criticizing you really matters. If it's someone in a professional setting, chances are they just have your best interests at heart, and want to see you grow and get better.

Ideally criticism should push and drive you to do better because you feel inspired and motivated. It took me a long time and like four improv classes to learn it.

But sometimes people <u>love</u> criticizing because it gives them a sense of power. They will find fault with anyone about anything. Tune these people out, because they don't care about your success - just your failures. They don't see all the parts of you that tried!

Criticism should not feel like it's coming from a place of shame.

Shame is not the best catalyst for moving forward! So if someone has you feeling down, it's OK to tune them out.

Another thing to take into account is if the person is criticizing something you did, or you as a person. This is hard because it can all feel personal! But there's a big difference between a teacher correcting a paper you wrote and a teacher saying you and your writing are terrible. Remember : good criticism is meant to be helpful and encourage growth!

let's make you stronger, because you can do this!

A great way criticism can be given is with the sandwich method. Start with a compliment, give a suggestion for improvement, and end with a compliment. I <u>HATE</u> giving criticism but we all are asked on occasion to do it, in work, school, and personal settings. Be kind about it, and people will respond to it.

I like the opening - maybe the middle part could be more organized so the amazing conclusion stands out!

that's helpful!

Criticism is hard. Criticism is scary. But you can survive it and continue to be an awesome person!

X WRONG!
You are so much more than someone's change, correction, or criticism

START OVER
You are a person who tried and maybe didn't succeed.

NO NO NO
You are HUMAN

TERRIBLE
And that is great!

HOW DO I DEAL WITH FEELING LIKE NOBODY NEEDS ME?

I am everything to everyone until I am nothing

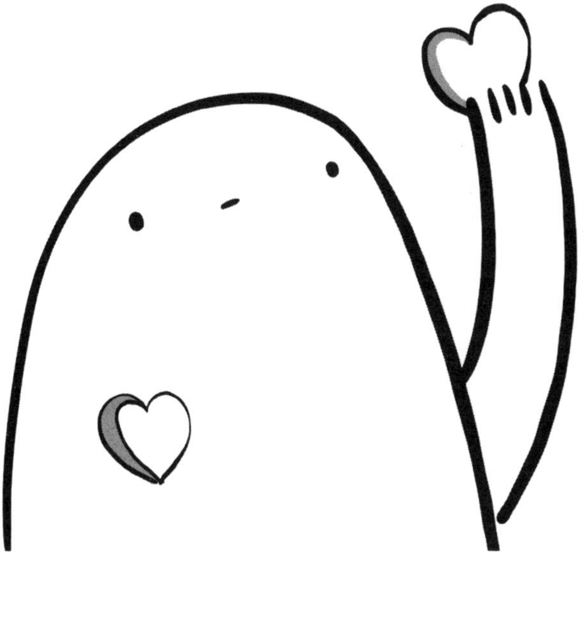

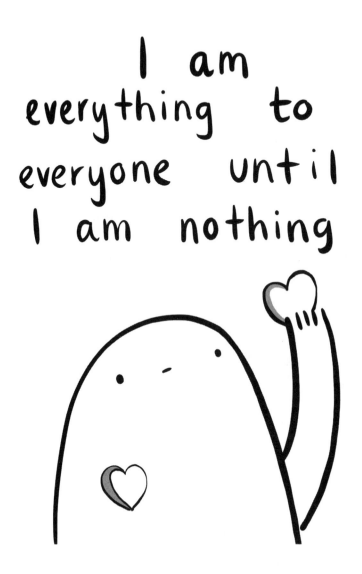

I have this horrible
need to be well
liked and loved
by everyone

this usually
means the following
tends to occur

I'll spend tons of time
making you
stuff

or send you
a text
because
I thought
of you

hey!
you!!!!

TUESDAY

X   X
I'll clear
my schedule
xx for you

FOR: YOU

and let you
into my corner
of the
world

and despite this, there is this cold
hard truth that keeps me up at
night, rattling through my head

they might not need
me as much as I
need them

I have to be totally loved by everyone or I freak out — and if there isn't constant reassurance, I want to combust

and if that affection isn't immediately returned in the same way, I come to this conclusion

EVERYONE HATES ME
NOBODY NEEDS ME
I AM THE WORST

Sometimes those worries about actually being needed really get me down, and I feel pretty alone in the scheme of things

Except... maybe I had been looking at it all wrong

maybe all my small actions were being returned

but in other ways

sometimes people show up for you in ways that aren't exactly like your own - if you're a talker about how much you care, maybe they show it by just being near you

this isn't bad - we just express it uniquely

and all those things you do for others? try doing them for yourself!

make something nice for yourself

give yourself small bits o' encouragement

I am OK

TUESDAY
✓
Make time for yourself ✓

♡

and love the world that's yours

It might not always feel like it, but people _do_ need you, and you need you too!
Because you're pretty darn cool

HOW DO I GET PAST A PERSONAL FAILURE?

We've all been there.

We've worked, tried, put effort in, and didn't succeed.

We've all failed.

And we've all OBSESSED over it.

People always say that failure is healthy
because it makes you work harder, etc.
I think these people tend to succeed a lot.
Success is sometimes harder for people,
and varies in all different areas of life.

And when you define all areas of your
life as needing to be successful all the
time, when you do fail it will HURT.
It's like, if I failed at this one area,
who says I won't fail in the others?

Here's the thing: Failure will happen. It will suck. You will beat yourself up. Accept that, and it will be easier to let it go. So, without further ado...

how to move past failure

EFFORT

Do you feel like you honestly did all you could but still failed? Good! Effort shows commitment and drive. It can feel wasted, but is totally a success in its own right. Trying is super amazing!

CIRCUMSTANCES

What was going on in life when you failed? Was it a hard time and were you asking a lot of yourself? Give yourself a break if things were really bad. We can only handle so much at a time.

CHANGES

Do you play the game of "I would do ___ differently?" Me too - I'm doing it with writing this book now!

Try to focus on applying it to future endeavors, instead of things you can't fix. I can't change what I put in this book, but I learned from my first book and put it in here ☺

Failure can make us not want to try or continue things, either because we did them and were terrible, or think if we try them we might be terrible. It's okay to feel this fear. You aren't a failure for being afraid of failing.

It helps to remember that failure can really feel like a mountain range. There are times when it feels like such a deep low that things will never pick up again. But things do change. And it's not one of those "choose to be happy" type of things. The world changes for bad and good all the time, and it's perfectly okay to want to roll with it until it feels better. Sometimes riding things out instead of trying to change every last thing can be so healthy.

Failures happen.

It's okay if you don't have it all figured out.

You are so much more than the things that didn't work out.

HOW DO I

CELEBRATE

MY SUCCESS?

On the flip side of failure,
there is the issue of success.

And there is a <u>LOT</u> to
worry about when something
goes right.

Take a deep
breath, because
you're going
to be okay.

Success can present the following big-time scary pressures:

what if EVERYTHING I do now has to be successful?

what if I can never be successful again and THIS IS IT?

what if even what I did was successful, but not even my full potential, so now I'm chasing this illusion of success for ever and ever, and I'm never completely happy with anything I do?

WHAT IF IT WASN'T EVEN A SUCCESS AND EVERYONE IS LYING TO MAKE ME HAPPY?

But hey, you did something right! You don't have to shout it from the rooftops, but you can appreciate what you've done.

If it's too much to acknowledge a big success, pick one thing about it that you did well and celebrate that!

And if you haven't experienced some big fancy success, take pride in your everyday success. How we treat people, ourselves, and the world are all little successes that matter in a big way. Don't discount them!

Sometimes thinking about success in the big scheme of things and life in general can be scary. But it also helps you figure out what's really important. How you define success and choose to remember it might change over time. Big or little, all kinds of victories, wins, and successes matter—because they are important to <u>you</u>.

TO DO + HAVE DONE

Sometimes this annoying guy shows up:

YOU DON'T DESERVE YOUR SUCCESS!

Oh man, this guy can go on and on about how you're a fake, how you didn't achieve anything, and everything about you is terrible. Long story short: HE IS THE WORST.

Here is something to keep in mind:

I did the thing, and you did not.

So stop.

He will start getting the picture — because by doing and living, we _are_ successes.

Success happens.

It's okay if you don't have it
all figured out.

You are so much more than the
events in your life.

HOW DO I APPROACH BEING CONFIDENT?

I CAN DO IT

Just be confident!

Just be quiet because it doesn't work like that!

Confidence is weird. It feels so... unnatural to me. I'm not someone who feels secure in ANY aspect of myself. So when people tell me "have some confidence!" I want to shrink and hide because I feel like I failed at that too!

come on!
Just believe in
your self!

nope
   never
no

Confidence isn't something you just magically get because someone told you to. It takes a long time to develop, and even longer to tell if you even believe it or not. Basically, it takes work.

oh no, I'm not going to pass

CONFIDENCE EXAM

With confidence, I'm a big believer of "fake it until you make it." Ironically my improv teacher always complained that I had no confidence – but I still loved playing characters. And that's what trying confidence is. You're playing a version of you that just has better self-esteem than usual.

okay, I <u>can</u> do this

It's a lot easier to actually put into practice than I am describing here. It's basically going into something scary (like a speech) and telling your awful inner voice "you are wrong, and we <u>can</u> do this, mostly because we have to, but also because we can."

so quiet down!

← mean inner voice

WAYS TO BE CONFIDENT

- tell yourself that even doing the things you're doing IS confidence
- nerves just show you care
- you're putting on a performance, and it's one of a lifetime
- engage with people, make eye contact, and be polite
- acknowledge that it COULD be worse, but it's not, so you're good
- pat yourself on the back for stepping outside your comfort zone

CONFIDENT PERSON IN TRAINING

You might not be confident in yourself

But I'm confident you are trying, and that you have <u>SO</u> many qualities beyond acting like you believe in yourself

It's OK to be quiet – all your good speaks for itself

Hard

Feelings

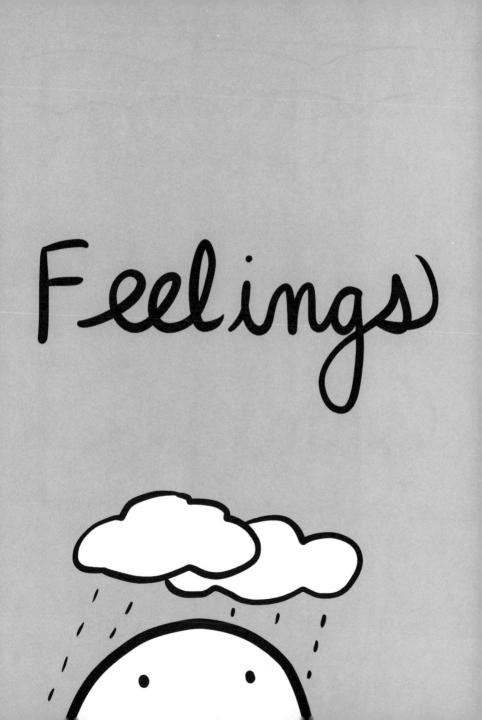

HOW DO I KNOW IF SOMETHING IS WRONG WITH ME?

IS IT IN MY HEAD?

sometimes when a lot of little things go wrong, it's hard to tell if they are going to morph into something else bigger and worse, or if they will remain slightly smaller and manageable.

and even the most seasoned mental health person can still wonder "is this really bad or just something I can handle on my own?"

so if this guy gets →

it might be time to talk to someone about how you feel (even though it's scary — because not doing anything will be even scarier...)

you crying more than usual

unusual eating

physical illness

isolating self →

disruption in sleep

bleak bleak bleak thoughts

Sometimes
we feel
steady

Sometimes we
feel off
balance

Sometimes
we feel very
much knocked
down

Sometimes we
really feel
like giving up

Sometimes we
pick ourselves
up when it's
super hard

Sometimes we
try and try
even though
everything feels
chaotic

Sometimes we

amaze ourselves

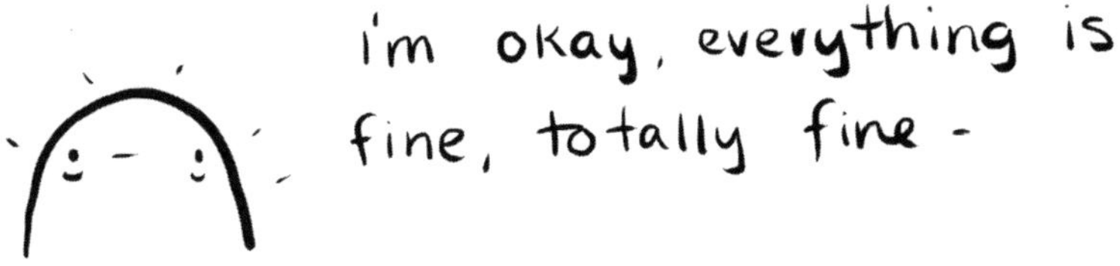
i'm okay, everything is fine, totally fine -

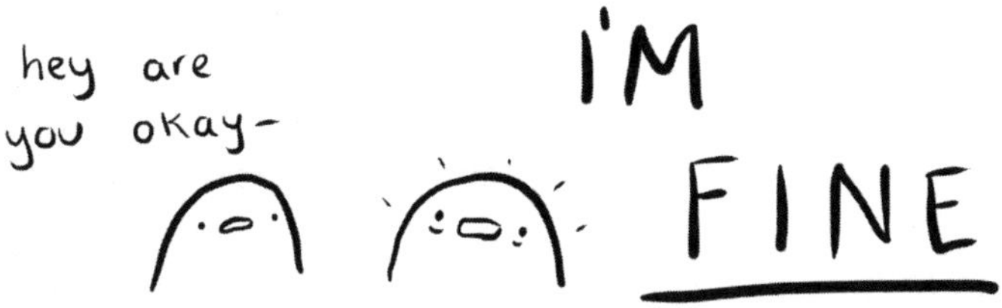
hey are you okay-
I'M FINE

If you are constantly telling yourself that everything is fine, things might not be so fine. You see, "fine" should be a state of being, not something you have to lie to yourself ten thousand times a day about.

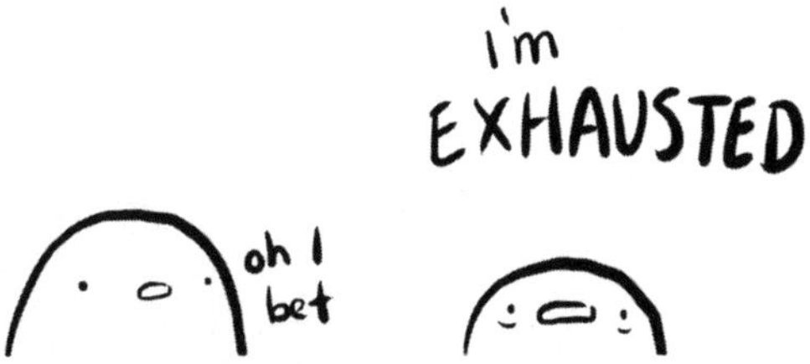
i'm EXHAUSTED
oh I bet

I'VE HAD ENOUGH

Everyone has their limits with life because life affects us all differently - it's good to know what yours might be

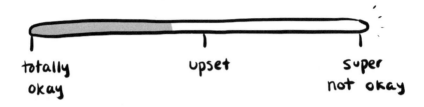

totally okay   upset   super not okay

A big part of taking care of yourself is knowing early on if you might be approaching hitting your limits - if you spend too much time feeling really not good, you might end up in a crisis situation, which is scary.

Take some time to recognize your limits- it's okay if you can't do everything!

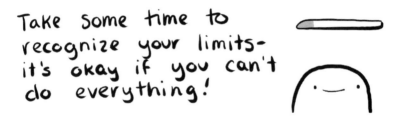

Just because you
feel bad and
lost doesn't
mean you're bad—
or can't be found

HOW DO I DEAL WITH EMOTIONAL DARK PITS?

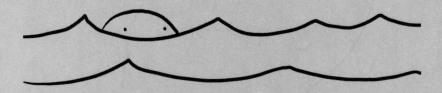

I am in
an emotional
dark pit

sinking

waiting

stuck

believe me -
I WANT OUT

But sometimes
people act like
I'm <u>choosing</u>
to be here

Dark pits are no fun - it's a keeping your head above water thing while you go through some of the worst times of  your life - no one would actively choose to do this

and, far too often, help can feel so out of reach

which leaves the task of treading waters and staying afloat up to you

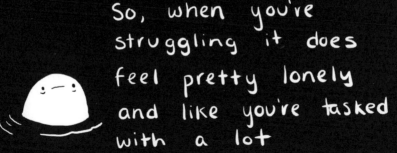

So, when you're struggling it does feel pretty lonely and like you're tasked with a lot

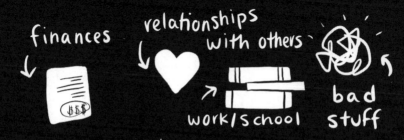

finances

relationships with others

work/school

bad stuff

Sometimes breaking down all the awful parts that make up the whole awful mess you're sinking in can give you clarity on what needs to be prioritized

As hard as it sounds, tackling problems a little bit at a time  will make it a little easier

ugh, let's start with you first...

you CAN do this dummy

There will be some pep talk

. you can't do ANYTHING dummy

And some negative talks

AHHHH

And some of... this

Hey, this stuff is hard!

But actively acknowledging the dark pit and trying to change it? That takes guts!

It's brave to try when things look bleakest

And while things might not look exactly how you want

you _will_ make it

HOW DO I STAY TOGETHER WHEN I FEEL LIKE I'M GOING TO PIECES?

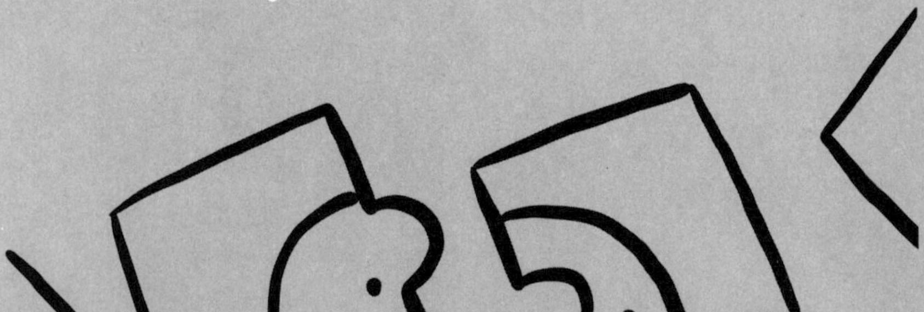

THINGS ARE GOING WRONG CHECKBOX

crying all the time	haven't left home in ages	loss of interest	out of body experiences
turning in work late	weird eating habits	constant panic attacks	too much TV, too little people time
hating? everything? ever???	SELF ISO-LATION!	general horrible misery	haha what are hobbies
ignoring everything (except maybe memes)	whatever this is	constant sleep	NO SLEEP EVER AGAIN!!!

★ If you are experiencing any of these feelings CONGRATULATIONS!!! Welcome to the Going To Pieces club!

going to pieces club

A group for people who feel like they're barely holding it together, and who feel like this quite a lot

great!

are you okay?

WE HAVE

- a lot of emotions
- self-doubt
- lingering fears
- FEELINGS

Join now and become a certified sad person who is trying to hold their life together

Somehow!

Okay, so feeling like this can be really difficult to manage, especially if you are trying to keep it all together on a daily basis.

It's not normal or healthy to feel like you're going to fall apart at any second. It's kind of normalized that we get pulled in a thousand different directions in life and call it a "balancing act" or whatever. A real balancing act should let you feel like a whole person who can meet the challenges of the day - not someone who might literally break in two.

So, the secret to keeping yourself from going to pieces isn't tape or anything to fix you up and keep going down whatever stressful path you're on — you really gotta find a path that isn't going to destroy you.

this is totally fine or something

YIKES

It's so so <u>so</u> important that you carve out time for yourself so you can deal with all the things that do stress you out. It sounds so clichéd, but when all the pieces of you are doing well, the pieces of life come together instead of falling apart.

ooooo h me time + self-care!

uhhhh I have five seconds to myself, I just want to breathe

I think there is also this idea that "me" time is an elaborate self-care ritual involving face masks and long baths. It's not everyone's thing. If you're happy just to have a few minutes to do whatever you want to do, that's so great! (Personally, I rant and rave in my diary and put stickers in it.)

It may feel like
everything is going
so wrong

It may feel like
you're not handling
it well

I'm trying

But you're doing what
you can and that
should totally be
recognized, you
amazing person!

HOW DO I HANDLE BEING ALONE?

ugh so many people

I can't wait to be alone

wait

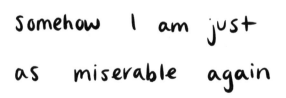

somehow I am just

as miserable again

ALONE.

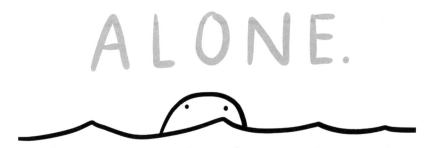

Whether we want to be or not, we all find ourselves alone sometimes. And that can be uncomfortable. Because even though we're by ourselves, it can be louder than ever, thanks to our noisy brains and anxious thoughts. Personally, I <u>HATE</u> being alone because all I do is ruminate on everything, and I get super worked up. Here is the worst stuff I do:

wonder what everyone else is up to

panic about stuff that will never happen

IMAGINARY BAD SITUATION

panic about stuff that hasn't happened yet

OCTOBER

worry that all these periods alone will last forever and ever

Learning to be by yourself is a skill like any other. It takes practice and effort to spend time by yourself and not want to go to pieces.

I struggle all the time, even if I carved out that alone time for myself.

Although phones keep us connected, checking social media can make us feel left out— and alone. Put the phone down and try living in the present moment.

If you really want or need to use the internet, try doing it on any device that's not your phone. It's easier to stay signed out of social media, and the lack of people texting you isn't an issue.

Get out and about for a bit. Sometimes just being around people in general feels less isolating. Libraries, shops, or just being outside can ease isolation.

Is there a hobby you keep meaning to try or continue? Now is a great time to explore that! It will keep you occupied and engaged, and your mind off things. Sometimes getting lost in a good book is just what you need.

If being alone is too much to bear, DO reach out for help. Being alone is a skill that takes time to develop.

can you help?

Alone time at best should feel rewarding and recharging — never so isolating that you want to fall apart

DOES REACHING OUT MAKE ME NEEDY? It can feel like it - but if you're honest about how you feel, your barrage of texts are likely forgiven.

some days are so
much lonelier than
others

keep treading those
scary waters - you're
so worth it

HOW DO I FIND COPING MECHANISMS I ACTUALLY LIKE?

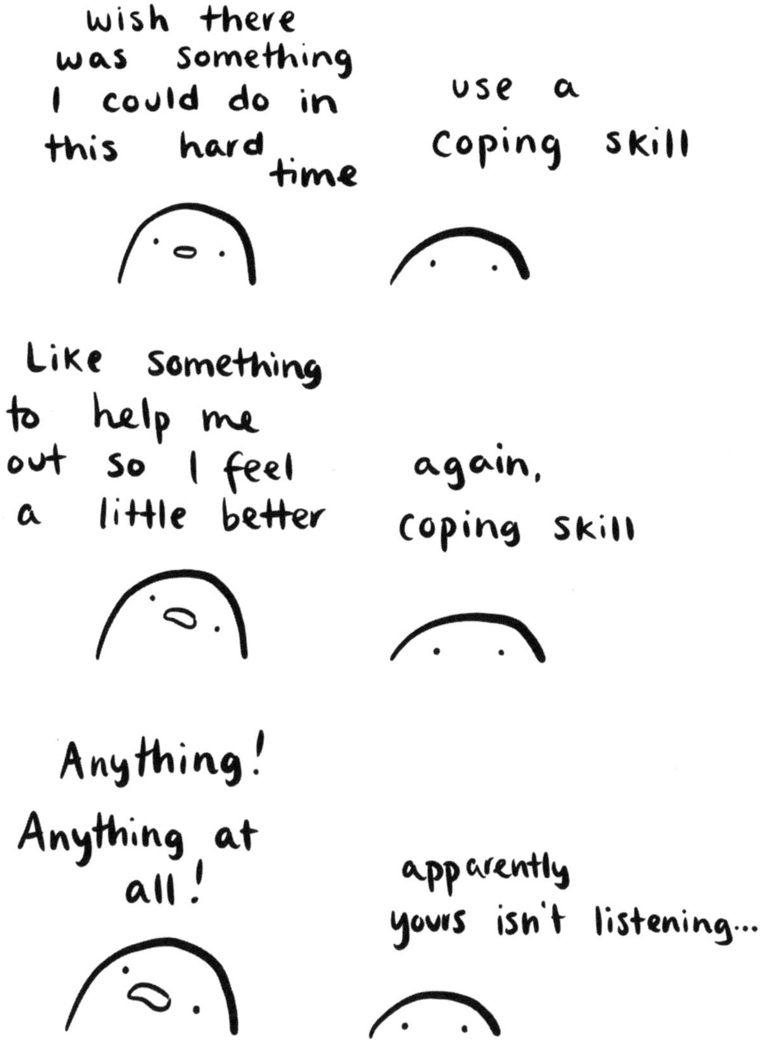
wish there was something I could do in this hard time
use a coping skill
Like something to help me out so I feel a little better
again, coping skill
Anything! Anything at all!
apparently yours isn't listening...

Coping mechanisms are pretty personal. Because of this, it can be pretty tricky trying to decide if one is right for you. There's A LOT out there, and everyone has their own feelings on them. And you do too.

It can feel a lot like this

Honestly, it's a lot of trial-and-error work. Unfortunately, there can be a lot of pressure on us if the first, second, tenth, or fiftieth thing doesn't work out.

Oh, that didn't work? But I thought-

— way too highly of that coping skill!

WHAT WORKS
These are just things I really like

A coping mechanism or skill should help you calm down a bit, make you feel safe and secure, and provide you with a sense of relief from your current panic or problems.

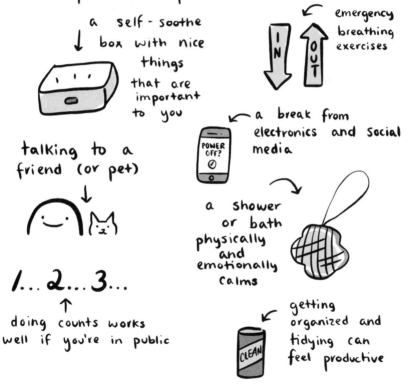

a self-soothe box with nice things that are important to you

emergency breathing exercises

IN OUT

a break from electronics and social media

POWER OFF?

talking to a friend (or pet)

a shower or bath physically and emotionally calms

1... 2... 3...

doing counts works well if you're in public

getting organized and tidying can feel productive

CLEAN

WHAT DOESN'T WORK
These are things I don't find super helpful

bottling ✓
it up
until it
hurts
too
much

There are lots of bad coping skills. We do a lot of them without even realizing it. These are some to maybe consider ditching or avoiding in the future.

alcohol, drugs,
and other numbing
solutions

DO
NOT
ENTER

✓ shutting
everyone out
when things
get bad

↓ physically abusing
your body (self-harm,
eating disorders, etc.)

UGH!
THE!
WORST!!!

↑
making cryptic
social media posts
about problems
and then deleting
them (it's just
unnecessary anxiety!)

We all cope in
different ways

It takes time to figure
out what works

Stay the course- you've
come so far already!

HOW DO I

DEAL WITH

GRIEF AND LOSS?

My world
has changed

I have changed

And I hurt
so
so
so
much

During the course of writing this book, I lost a family member and my cat. It's been difficult, overwhelming, and a wild bunch of emotions. And it's hard. It's hard because people often expect grief to look one way:

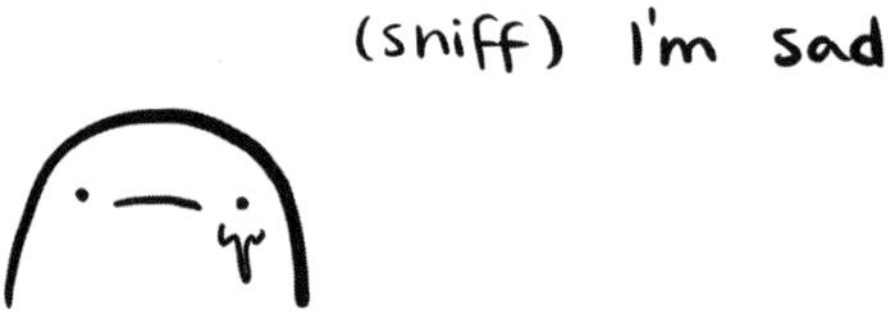
(sniff) I'm sad

But it can really look (and feel) like **A LOT**:

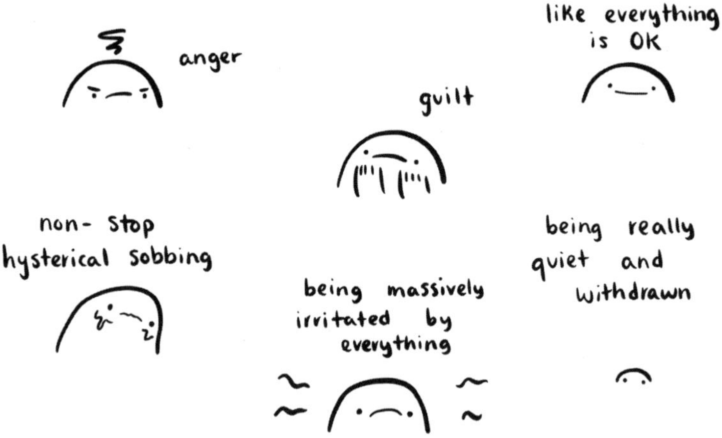
anger
guilt
like everything is OK
non-stop hysterical sobbing
being massively irritated by everything
being really quiet and withdrawn

Basically, if it's an emotion, you might feel it.

Sometimes people treat person-loss and pet-loss differently. I think it all depends on what your relationship was like. But in the end, loss is loss, and it all totally hurts.

pet-loss can be SO PAINFUL, and don't let anyone diminish your feelings on it. Pets matter so much!

The worst part is the only thing that ever helps — time. Those horrible feelings really only quiet down after many days and nights. Be gentle to yourself and give yourself the gift of time to heal. There's no magic calendar date to it. Just your strength.

Tuesday

GET BETTER?

Some people don't deal with loss right away. It may hit them days, weeks, or even years later. It's okay, because grief isn't logical. You'll unpack it when you're ready to.

There can be a LOT of pressure to deal with it all immediately

GRIEF

Don't rush it. Really. It's better to wait if you need more time

There's no right or wrong way to deal with grief and its fallout. There's only you and what you need to get through this hard time. It will be scary, sad, and suck big time. But you can come out on the other side—hurt, but still here.

Will things be normal again? Maybe. But it's also okay if there's a new normal too.

Getting through grief isn't always
like this

Sometimes it's a lot of this

Whatever yours looks like, it's
fine - you're getting through, and
that is so strong and brave

that's
you
↓

being so
awesome!

HOW DO I BOUNCE BACK AFTER A HARD TIME?

I'm
trying to
get back
to life

I'm finding my
way out

But hard stuff
still sometimes
lingers

If you've been through something big and are now ready to immerse yourself back in life, it can be... daunting. A lot has probably changed. you've probably changed too. And you might have some worries about that.

what if everyone thinks there's something wrong with me?

what if I let people down?

what if I end up back where I started?

what if I can't cope with sliding into my old routine?

No matter what happened, it's okay that it affected you - and still affects you. Hard times are HARD. There's often no right or wrong way to come back. It takes such courage, strength, and heart to do.

it's like being a real - life super hero, being so brave!

Bouncing back to life takes time. Like, a lot of it. Almost annoyingly so. Trying to fit into your routine again feels so weird, like a jigsaw puzzle in the wrong place. You just want to make it work, but can't.

Sometimes you <u>have</u> to slow it down and not rush it. It sucks, I know. But try to figure out what you need today, right now, in this moment. It's so easy to get caught up in long term plans. But nurturing in the here and now can set up long term success. Take a deep breath - you've got this.

It's important to be gentle with yourself during this transition time. You're bridging the gap between a major event and daily life. "Be gentle" is thrown around a lot, but can include:

- giving yourself permission to struggle

- not beating yourself up over every little mistake

- accepting your limitations

- not tackling too much at once

- giving yourself space to reflect and proccess things

- listening to your body's needs

These are hard and challenging things.

It's okay.

You're okay.

Bouncing back takes
time and effort

You're so worth it

Bounce onward, upward,
and higher than before!

Self

Care

HOW DO I STAY POSITIVE?

everything is great
or something yay?!?

Wheel of Positivity

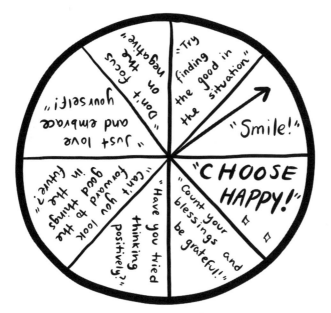

Or, STOP TELLING ME THESE THINGS WHEN I AM CLEARLY STRUGGLING!

If you have ever been sad before, you've probably heard this gem:

why can't you just be happy? like, just think positive!

This can really put a damper on any and all notions related to positivity. Like, you want to destroy the word itself. Because it represents this awful, totally unobtainable thing that feels impossible.

I'm the POSITIVITY MONSTER and I demand you love yourself and all aspects of your life! Fear me and my power of only thinking nice thoughts!

ugh, not you...

Positivity can feel positively impossible, and that's okay! No one has the capacity to feel good every minute of the day. Bad things happen, and feelings get tricky. It's OK to acknowledge and really feel those feelings.

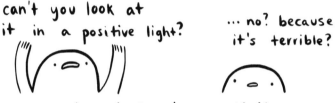

can't you look at it in a positive light?

... no? because it's terrible?

You can also look at positivity as not sunshine and rainbows, but as a feeling of "at least it isn't as bad as it was."

see your inner beauty! love all you do! choose happy!

at least I'm not actively destroying my life as much anymore

Don't sweat it if you aren't meeting everyone else's definitions of positivity. You look at the world through your own view. And that's pretty cool!

feel good!

THINK POSITIVE!

HAVE A GOOD ATTITUDE!

look forward to the future

???

that's a little hard due to things

I'm going through — like I can't think that way right now, okay?

... Maybe you can take things a day at a time. Like feeling good about everything doesn't happen overnight.

that's true

You might feel good about everything, or maybe some things, or maybe nothing. It's okay, you're figuring things out. I hope you find some level of joy that makes your days feel whole and you a little more complete!

thanks, you too!

HOW DO I STAND UP FOR MY PERSONAL BELIEFS?

you are my personal beliefs

♡ hey!

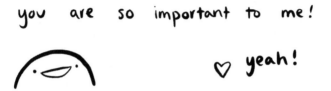

you are so important to me!

♡ yeah!

I can't wait to share you with the world!

♡ uh...

INTERNET vs REALITY

When discussing personal beliefs, they can be very close to our hearts. But if it's the internet or reality, talking about these things can have very different responses and reactions...

Some people can be loud and mean online, but calm in life

And some can be calm online, but so loud in life

Some are just always calm

And some... yeah... are like <u>that</u>

What makes talking about our personal beliefs so hard is that they're __PERSONAL__.

That's okay, because it shows you care about what you believe in. Caring is never a bad thing.

I care about this thing so much but I don't always know how to express that

Sometimes it's hard to talk about what we believe in because we're afraid people might look down on us, judge us, or worst of all - start an argument with us.

This is important to me and a part of my identity

UGH.
BE. ASHAMED.

(Sadly this seems to happen a lot when you talk about basic human rights. Remember, everyone deserves human rights! ♡)

WAYS TO STAND UP
FOR WHAT YOU BELIEVE IN

get involved with people who share your beliefs!

Attend events and volunteer- help is always appreciated

If someone is actively dissing everything you believe in, it's OK to say something - people are suprisingly receptive to talking in real life

But **NEVER** do that if you're uncomfortable or in danger. You're one person, and not responsible for the entire world.

The internet can be a great place to connect, but it's OK to disconnect if it seems like it's making your beliefs feel constantly under scrutiny.

Our beliefs live and thrive in our hearts, and not in the comments of strangers.

you have your own
unique voice

sometimes it feels like no
one wants to hear it

but it's yours, and it's
awesome!

HOW DO I LOVE MYSELF?

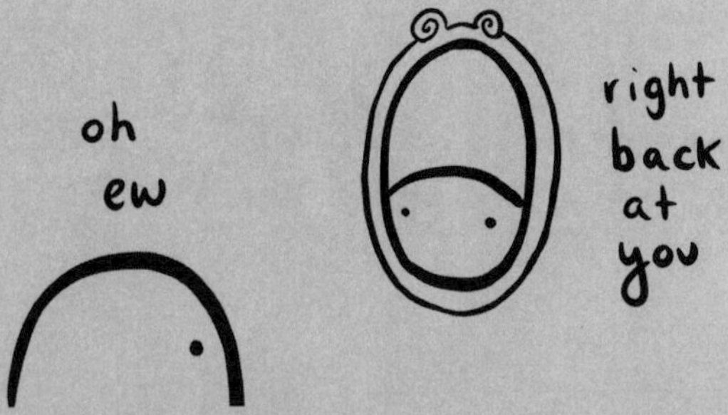

In many ways, I am both the totally wrong and right person to ask this question to:

On the wrong side, I have major self-esteem issues and a horrible eating disorder

On the right side, I know how tremendously hard it is to live with — and love — yourself.

"LOVE YOURSELF" is HARD.

It's a statement that puts a lot of pressure on yourself. Personally, I see "loving" yourself in two ways.

MIND

✔ What goes on in your head- personality, thoughts, actions, likes, quirks, etc.

BODY

And these two guys? They **NEVER** agree.

What you physically look like - and what the world sees.

MIND

All your thoughts and opinions make you, well, you.

And that's okay. No one's minds are identical, and everyone has their own thoughts going on.

Appreciating all your big wild brain does takes some practice. Like it controls your breathing and bodily functions and still has time to give you a personality? Wild. Pausing and reflecting that it has a massive job to do and that you still have to be a whole functioning person makes it a little easier. Do you have to love your whole mind and all the things that rattle around in it that sometimes make your life hard? No! Just understand that both of you are trying your best.

BODY

Things get hard here, because while you can't open up your mind and yell at it, you can touch and feel your body and be totally hideous to it. You can be downright horrible to yourself and do a lot of damage. And it's so easy to feel like you're a failure. Tack on forced self-love and it's a disaster.

I'm currently struggling with an eating disorder that is totally impacting all parts of my life. It's so hard to want to be kind to my body when even eating is a huge battle.

I'm trying to appreciate its mechanics, like that it takes me places and lets me do things. I need my body to live.

Sometimes I try to be nice to my body when I'm also being horrible to it. Simple acts like brushing my teeth or trying a new shampoo are small ways to stay in touch when I feel that huge disconnect.

You don't have to love every inch of yourself. But you do need a body to live. Sometimes the best we can manage when we're at war with ourselves is a truce.

And that's okay. You're okay.

SELF-LOVE IS A LIE.

You don't need to love yourself unconditionally to deserve love from other people. You don't need to be comfortable in your own skin to be worthy of good things. Everyone is worthy of love, respect, and success in life. So no matter how you feel right now, just know you deserve good things, regardless of your opinion of yourself.

It can also feel like you spend all your time chasing self-love but it never seems to click. That's okay! It might never be to the point where you're like "wow, every part of me is awesome!" But being able to maybe acknowledge you have some good things about yourself is amazing. Don't be too hard on yourself if you're struggling.

You know how people are like "Don't do it for other people, do it for yourself"? I think it's okay to want to do certain things for other people. If the people around you encourage, motivate, and want you to be happy and healthy, **GO FOR IT!** Especially if you're in a hard place and trying to get better! Those around us can be great at seeing things about ourselves that we can't always see. And sometimes we have to find ourselves along the way when we're on difficult paths.

me

my best friend, Eli, who is helping me a ton with my eating disorder

slow down

take a breath

you're only one person,
and you don't have to
be perfect

you're you

and I

like that

HOW DO I SHOW KINDNESS TO MYSELF?

BE KIND TO YOURSELF!

what no

ew gross

BE! KIND! TO! YOURSELF!!!

nope

SELF-KINDNESS!

why?!?

Self-Kindness can be a mystery. Especially when we're at war with ourselves. Like, me? ME? I deserve Kindness?!? And trying to demonstrate it to ourselves is impossible!

what no go away ♡

I think one way to practice being kind to ourselves is by being kind to others. Sometimes we see value in others before we can see it in ourselves. And that's okay - being in tune with other's needs and feelings can help us identify those same things in ourselves.

It's not bad to care about other people — and it's not bad to care about yourself. It's always okay and good to care! I promise!

Another way to be kind to yourself is by paying attention to your body's physical and emotional needs. Need some sleep or a good cry? Give it a go. Indulge yourself.

you can sleep-cry

it's ok!

And so much of self-kindness seems tied up with self-love. Almost like you have to love yourself to deserve kindness. Which totally isn't the case! Think of it this way: if a friend was struggling, would they deserve to be treated horribly? Of course not! You don't have to love yourself, but you do need to get along to some degree to keep going.

we're in this together

yeah

And while doing some impulse purchases might seem like a way to be kind to yourself, there's plenty of nonmonetary options:

↑
exploring your feelings through journaling

making a sleep pattern that works for you

↓

↑
spending time indoors or outdoors - wherever you feel the most comfortable

↑
and if you do impulse-purchase, try a plant!

Saying you will be kind
to yourself is easy

Putting it into practice
is hard

Don't give up on it — you've
totally got this!

Change

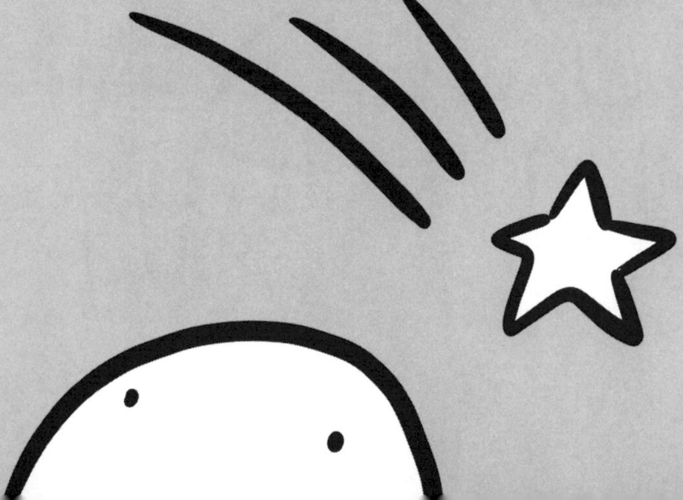

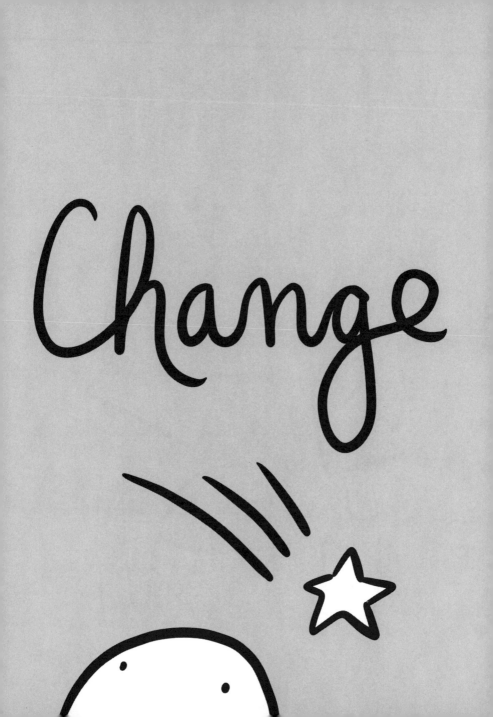

HOW DO I CHANGE?

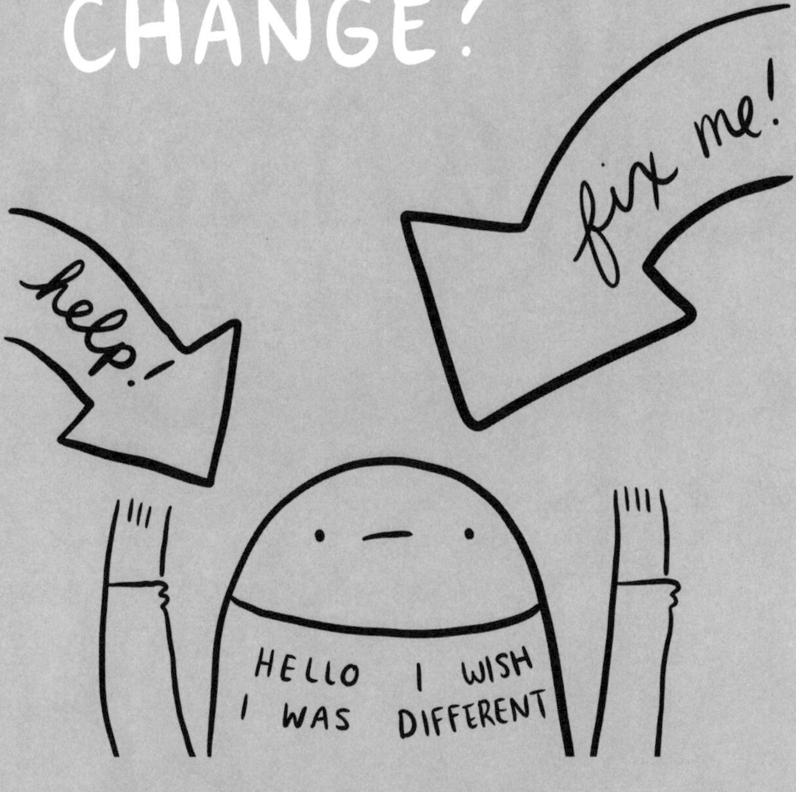
help!
fix me!
HELLO I WISH
I WAS DIFFERENT

Sometimes we get
the notion that
maybe - just maybe -
we'd like to change

Maybe there's
an external
reason why

Maybe we
have no choice
but to change

Or maybe we
just decided
we want to

Change isn't easy. It's scary. And it's frightening deciding "Hey, I _do_ need things to be different." Because they will be different. And it will be hard and difficult and you will question everything you do. But the best change happens when we aren't even paying attention. It seamlessly blends into our lives and we just live. Let's take a look at some strategies for starting and not totally hating change ⟶

WHAT DO I WANT TO CHANGE?

SCHOOL / JOB

We all get the urge to just quit and start over. It's totally natural! If you really want to, figure out an exit plan and a timeline. Sometimes just doing this helps us decide if we really want quit everything, or if we need to reorganize what we're doing and stick with where we're at. Just playing with our options can be helpful.

SOCIAL LIFE

Wanting to make new friends or change friend groups is hard, but sometimes necessary. Relationships sometimes fade but also abruptly end. It's okay to evaluate these relationships. Figure out who is important, and spend time with them. Pull back from the people who drain you. You'll find your rhythm.

APPEARANCE

Being at war over your looks can be so hard and so damaging. It's okay if you hate the way you look and hate the idea of self-love. Don't feel bad for feeling bad. But maybe talk to someone about how you're feeling. It can be really isolating and hard to deal with by yourself, and can lead to big problems. So try to reach out!

EVERYTHING

Life can be so overwhelming and nauseating that we want to hit a reset button, crawl out of our own skin, and just be a totally different person than who we've always been.

It's okay. It happens and it sucks. Don't feel guilty for wanting to just quit your life. But just know there are a <u>lot</u> of us out there who feel the same way. We know and totally get that pain. There's no one right solution to this problem...

...but talk to someone. Let them know what's happening. It's cliche'd, but it's also better than just sitting with a knot in your stomach watching the same things continue to unfold while you're miserable. Even just verbalizing it can be a huge relief, and help you get through another day.

Life shouldn't be about getting through days. You should be comfortable being an active participant. I hope you get there!

Setting __realistic__ expectations helps make change more achievable and rewarding. Hitting those baby steps makes accomplishing big stuff so much easier.

you'll want to measure your progress every day - it's natural. But big changes rarely happen overnight. Don't stress if you can't see a difference immediately - there's so much you're doing already.

And if the idea of the long term is way too stressful, try thinking about what you can do today - and only today - that's different.

Breaking down change a bit at a time is a little less stressful. It will never be a stress-free thing, but this might help minimize how overwhelming it can be.

We can grow and change

We can do it
at our own
pace

You've got this!

HOW DO I HANDLE EVERYTHING AROUND ME CHANGING?

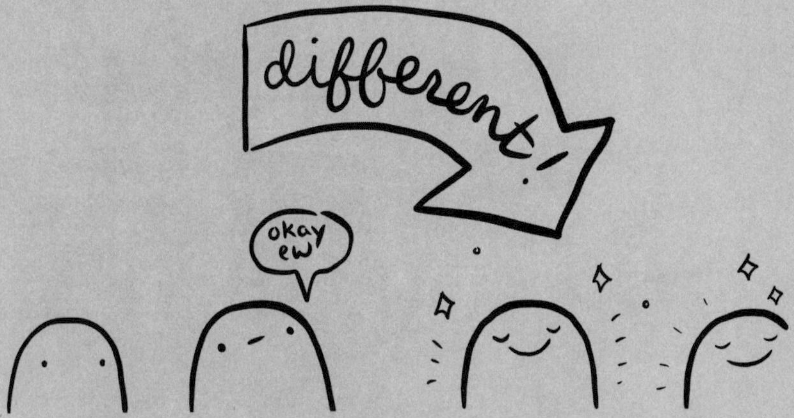

EVERYTHING CHANGING

CAN BE UPSETTING

Seriously, change is always made out to be this really exciting thing, but the majority of the time I want to scream, because **I HATE IT.**

Everything is out of my control and different! Why would anyone ever like that?!?

I barely have my current stuff under control AND NOW IT'S ALL CHANGING

AHHHHH!

EXAMPLES OF CHANGE THAT CAN BE HARD

- major life milestones (weddings, births, etc.)
- major life disruptions (divorce, death)
- moving anytime ever
- major life transitions (graduation)
- really good stuff like vacations but you're still miserable because ROUTINE DISRUPTION!
- getting a job
- losing a job
- stuff that is unannounced but you can feel it, like gaining or losing friendships
- RELATIONSHIPS!!!
- just the general feeling of change

It doesn't matter if it's a good change or a bad change – you're totally allowed to feel yucky about change because it's one of the hardest parts of being human

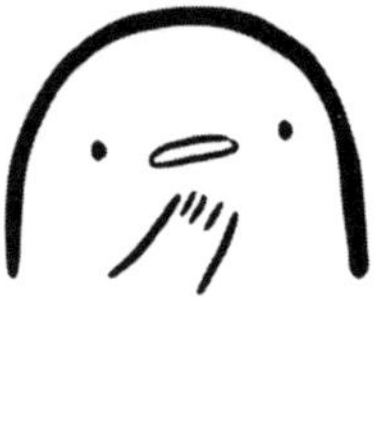

LET'S COPE!

People are always like "Embrace the change!" Well, that's a lot to ask of someone. So let's cope.

Lifestyle

Sometimes our environment changes and it's stressful. We change schools or jobs or graduate or move.

And it is HARD.

to adore your new surroundings, but making a small list of one thing you like about it every day can make it a little easier to adjust.

People

I really struggle when I feel like people are changing because I feel like they'll decide they don't need me anymore and abandon me. Self-isolating doesn't help, but do try reaching out and staying connected. People may change and leave, but your awesome qualities are always there to stay ♡

MORE COPING!

(ACTIVE COPING!)

flashback

Is there a time in your life that did feel good and comforting? Play some music from that time, or watch some TV you enjoyed. Connecting with your positive past can keep you grounded.

future

It's OK to embrace things to come too. Adding small new things to your life, like a plant, a new recipe, or nail polish can make being in the moment a little easier.

in the moment

So sometimes it's ridiculously hard to appreciate anything going on when your life really sucks. That's fine - just remember to keep in touch with the things that <u>do</u> matter, like friends, family, pets, or whatever form of media is your current obsession. It will help you feel more like you.

go ahead, cry!

Your tears are totally fine and help relieve pent up stress and anxiety. And sometimes you do feel a lot better from it. Letting your emotions out can totally help your health in the long run. But if you can't stop crying all the time, don't be afraid to reach out for help dealing with change. (I've been there myself.)

things can change

people can change

you can change —
        or not

you can be the
you that <u>you</u>
            want

HOW DO I

STOP FOCUSING

ON THE PAST?

FRIENDS
RESPONSIBILITIES
SCHOOL
FAMILY
I'm struggling to cope!
WORK

Oh, not you too!
THE PAST

Even though we know we're living in the present, sometimes our minds want us living in the past. Maybe things were easier then- or maybe they were so painful we can't forget. Either way, the past can be super invasive and can stop us from living in the now.

come onnnnn!
let's go!
sigh...
the past

And honestly, it can feel like this constant torment that leaves you with zero clear plan for moving forward. It's that being trapped between the past and future that is so anxiety- inducing.

ugh!
past
future
more future

When the past takes hold, it's pretty powerful. logically you know you want to move forward, but you're so, so stuck. You're not alone in this, and there are some ways to un- stick yourself from all this...

Sometimes looking at the past can be a good thing, because we can see how much actually has changed. We're always changing, and that isn't always visible to us. But actually looking back and acknowledging that change - for good or for bad - has occurred lets us feel more grounded in the time we're currently living in.

You know how some people are like "I'm so glad (bad event) happened because it made me stronger"? yeah I really hate that kind of thinking too. Just know you should never feel pressure to love and appreciate everything that's happened to you. Feel free to hate it — and take what you've learned with you as a means to move forward. It can be a good or bad lesson, it doesn't matter. Just know you want things to be different.

THE PAST

hey, I need advice

sure!

When we're caught up in bad stuff from the past and it feels so overwhelming, sometimes I imagine what opposite me would do. Like, if I never experienced (x), what would I do in (y) situation? Sure, people say don't play "what if" with the past. But if I am going to do it, I might as well inch forward - just a little.

YOU DON'T OWN ME!

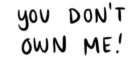

I literally define all the reasons why you do any actions on any given day?....

yeah, no, you're right

We have a lot of parts to us,
past, present, and future

Knowing where we come from
helps us figure out where to go

Don't worry about the journey-
you'll get there, and
you've got this!

HOW DO I THINK ABOUT THE FUTURE?

(AND NOT CRY?)

you know when everything is falling apart but someone wants to make plans for months from now, or wants to know what you'll be up to in your school/ work/love life?

can I pencil
you in for next May?

... you "may" not

yeah, it's THE WORST.

Unfortunately a lot of people like planning ahead, and assume we'll all run on the same planning and commitment schedule that they like to keep. And it's so, so hard to deal with constant planning when even thinking ahead to the next few days is so hard.

TUESDAY

It's okay to acknowledge that the future might be unplanned or unsteady or even just plain miserable. We're human, and things happen — especially things that make us dread the future.

Anyone who is nonstop excited for the next year or two has <u>totally</u> felt this way before. We all have.

future

I think it sometimes helps to acknowledge these things:

1. The future is coming
2. It's OK to be scared
3. I don't have to have everything sorted out right this second today
4. I will take things one day at a time so I am not overwhelmed
5. I am one person who can only do so much

"TAKE IT A DAY AT A TIME..."

People will tell us this, but what does it really mean to do so?

Figure out what can be accomplished today- and only work on that.

And if it helps, make a list of stuff that can be dealt with LATER.

Pick one thing that will make today worthwhile. A small reward like reading a book or going to a store you like can help you get through the day a little bit happier.

If you didn't have a good day, it's okay. You get another brand-new day tomorrow. And you can start over, try again, and feel cleansed. You've got this!

REMEMBER: IT'S ONE DAY, NOT FOREVER!

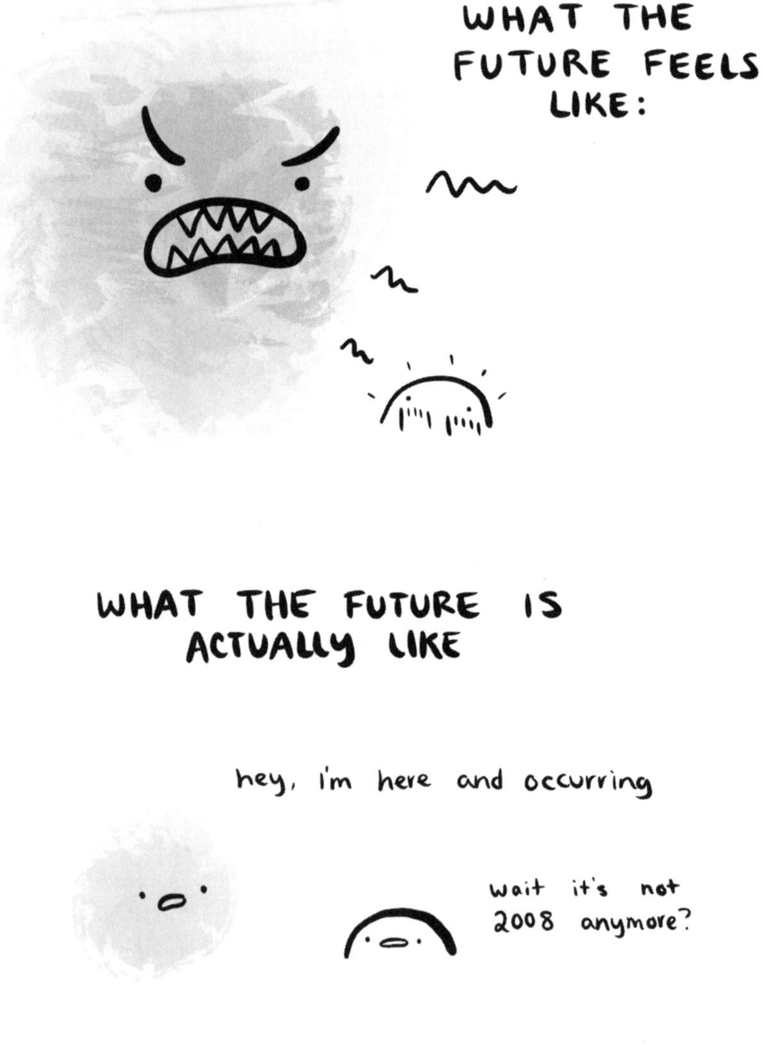
WHAT THE FUTURE FEELS LIKE:
WHAT THE FUTURE IS ACTUALLY LIKE
hey, i'm here and occurring
wait it's not 2008 anymore?

People always want to know
where you will be in
the future —

What you'll be doing, who
you'll be with...

Mostly, I just want
to be happy.

HOW DO I

(EMOTIONALLY)

MOVE?

THIS
END UP
OR WHATEVER

Moving is a REALLY big change, and even if it's five minutes or five hours away, it can be stressful, exhausting, and push you to the brink.

whether it's your first move or 50th - it takes so much out of you...

I think it really boils down to one concept: EVERYTHING IS DIFFERENT AND NOT WHAT I'M USED TO. Being taken out of your normal element can be really hard.

where did I put that?

I know where it is at my old place!

where's my sweater?

Did I just lose half of my stuff?

I can't find anything!

But sometimes our hearts hurt because we miss our old place too. It's okay. Old homes represent a lot — events, good and bad memories— a whole chapter of our lives.

So while being smart about packing and organizing your essentials can be really helpful and decrease some stress, acknowledging the emotional toll can make things suck a little less too. I have moved twice in under two years, and each time it's been a really big adjustment for me. I struggle immensely with it. And it always feels like the end of the world!

everything around me is different - will I be different too? Am I really ready for that?

Moving On

I like printing photos of my old places and of times from when I lived there. I keep some on my phone too. It just reminds me it's **OK** to remember it all.

Taking the time to hang up a favorite picture or put a plant out makes a new place feel like you remember your home - but is also a step toward embracing your new place too.

Sometimes it's hard trying to love everything about your new location. Taking some walks helps you get adjusted, but also lets you find new things to love. It will take time, and that's okay!

NEW st.

If you're making a change with who you live with (like going from roommates to by yourself) it is HARD. And a super weird change! Allow yourself time to adjust to this, because it will be tough for a while. I had this happen and it was hard. I worked through some of this by doing cleaning and organizing, trying new craft projects, and ALWAYS leaving the TV on - it helped me feel a little less lonely.

ALONE

It does take a while
for places to feel like
home

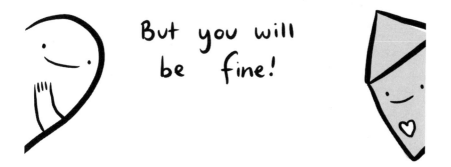

But you will
be fine!

You will fit into your home -
and your home will fit into <u>you</u>

HOW DO I

SHOW PEOPLE

I AM CHANGING?

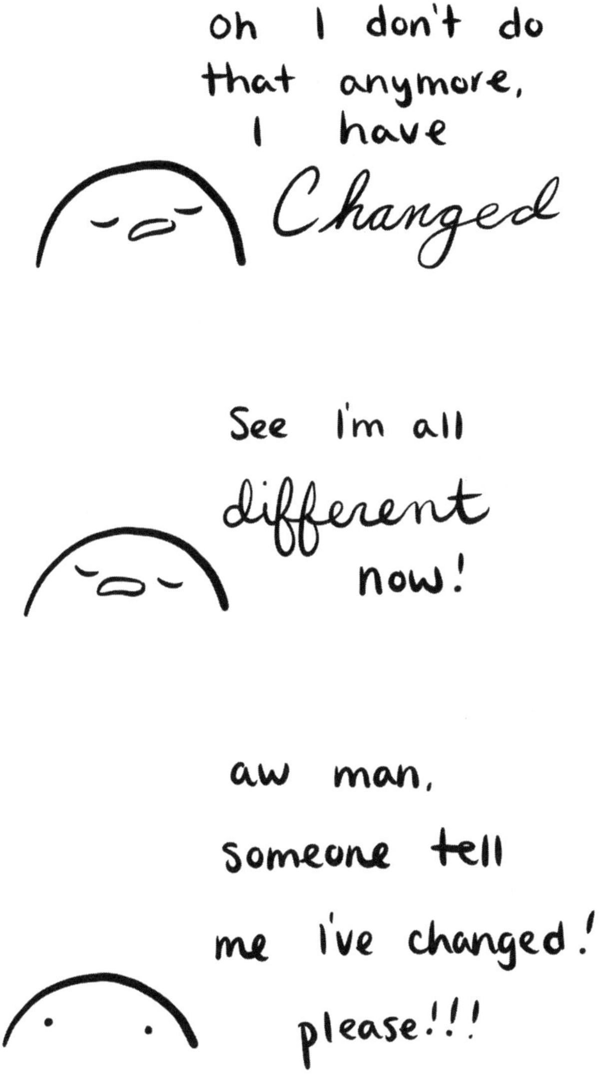
Oh I don't do that anymore, I have Changed
See I'm all different now!
aw man, someone tell me I've changed! please!!!

Sometimes when we're trying to get better, be different, or make a switch, we are totally desperate to show people we're trying to change. Like, "hey, look at me! It's me not doing that stuff I used to do!"

haha wow I sure am better, now!

In our quest to show these changes we can put a lot of pressure on ourselves. Pressure like "I'll never cry in front of anyone again!" This is unfair to ourselves. Change isn't always about being perfect or never feeling sad again. It's more about <u>how</u> we deal with those things.

Maybe instead of bawling and saying "I'm fine!" you actually say what's wrong - that's change, baby!

We can say "I've changed!" until we are blue in the face, but most people want to __see__ change. And that's tricky, because you can't pull change out of thin air. It takes time to show and demonstrate actual change.

maybe you try group events

or someone sees you take your medication

or that you're doing hobbies / relaxing

It sucks we feel the need to prove change, and we shouldn't have to in the first place. But the best way to do so is to live your life. Do the things that make you, well, you. Use the things you've learned to carve out the life you want. People will catch up in time and see all your progress!

I'm proud!

Thanks!

WHAT IF NO ONE NOTICES?

There's one of two things with this:

1. They truly don't notice

2. They notice, but don't want to say anything and make you uncomfortable

It can be so hard when all of our work goes totally unnoticed or unappreciated. So, I will say to you - I notice! You have been doing an amazing job through some really hard times, and you will continue to do great! And if you stumble I know you'll find your way back - because you've been doing so well!

It's so hard to believe in yourself - but I believe in you!

a crown for you

SELF-CHANGING CHAMPION

It's nice to show other
people you're changing

It's nice to show yourself
you're changing too

Keep up the good work!

ACKNOWLEDGMENTS

I'd like to thank everyone over at William Morrow for all their amazing work throughout the whole writing, editing, and publishing process. Liate Stehlik, Benjamin Steinberg, Cassie Jones, Susan Kosko, Andrew DiCecco, Pamela Barricklow, Andrea Molitor, Leah Carlson-Stanisic, Jeanne Reina, Andrew Gibeley, and Amelia Wood are the best starting lineup anyone could ask for.

I'd also like to thank editors old and new—Emma Brodie, who has helped me so much over the years with putting books together, and Vedika Khanna, who has been absolutely invaluable, insightful, and extraordinary throughout the editing process. I'm so excited for both of your futures.

Special thanks to my agent, Penny Moore, who has been such a guiding light throughout the whole wild publishing process—thanks for having faith in me, and for all the wonderful work you've been doing in the world. We need more people like you. Thanks also go to Chelsey Heller and Erin Files in foreign rights.

I would also like to thank my friend and fellow writer/illustrator Tyler Feder, who sat with me in cafés all around Chicago, read all of my rough drafts, and generally made me feel like I could actually do this. I'm so proud of how far both of us have come.

I'd also like to thank my therapist, Samantha, for giving me the courage to see this project through, and helping me to learn to value myself in ways other than my jeans size.

I would also like to thank my improv group for pushing me forward to at least pretend I am confident, but for also pushing me to be me. Late nights in Chicago will always hold a place in my heart. Special thanks to Kelly, Sompong, and Shreya for being so amazing.

Extra-special thanks to Eli, who is the best friend anyone could ask for, and who wasn't afraid to see the real me in Seattle.

Special thanks go to my mom, dad, and brother, for always sticking around when things get tough, and for loving me always. Double thanks to my cats Chloe and Sammy, who I love to pieces.

Finally, thank you to everyone who has read my work, supported me, and taken the time to write to me about their own experiences. I really can't put into words how much all of this means to me, and you're all treasures.

HarperCollins books may be purchased for educational, business, or sales promotional use. For information, please email the Special Markets Department at SPsales@harpercollins.com.

FIRST EDITION

Library of Congress Cataloging-in-Publication Data has been applied for.

ISBN 978-0-06-298367-1

20 21 22 23 24   LSC   10 9 8 7 6 5 4 3 2 1